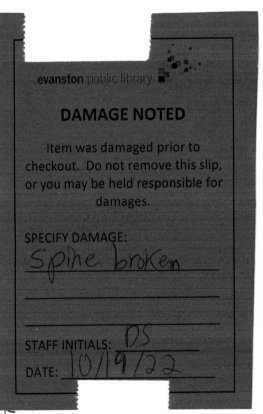

WRITING the MEMOIR

WRITING

the

MEMOIR

From Truth to Art

J<small>UDITH</small> B<small>ARRINGTON</small>

The Eighth Mountain Press
Portland, Oregon 1997

An excerpt from Chapter 9, "Writing about Living People," was first published in the July 1996 special issue of *The Women's Review of Books,* "The Memoir Boom." Permissions acknowledgments appear on page 181.

Cover design by Marcia Barrentine
Book design by Marcia Barrentine and Ruth Gundle

Manufactured in the United States of America
This book is printed on acid-free paper.
First edition 1997
10 9 8 7 6 5 4 3 2 1

LIBRARY OF CONGRESS CATALOGING-IN-PUBLICATION DATA
Barrington, Judith.
    Writing the memoir : from truth to art / Judith Barrington. — 1st ed.
        p.   cm.
    Includes index.
    ISBN 0-933377-41-X (lib. trade : alk. paper). — ISBN 0-933377-40-1 (alk. paper)
    1. Autobiography — Authorship. 2. Biography as a literary form.
    I. Title
    CT25.B285   1997
    808'.06692—dc20   96–43065

THE EIGHTH MOUNTAIN PRESS
624 Southeast Twenty-ninth Avenue
Portland, Oregon 97214
phone: (503) 233-3936
fax: (503) 233-0774

For Will,
who wanted to hear the true stories

Table of Contents

Acknowledgments

Grateful thanks to Andrea Carlisle, writer, teacher, and friend, who read the manuscript of this book and gave me invaluable help. She challenged my assumptions about memoir, debated questions of truth, and helped me find out what I believe about all this.

Also of great help were discussions I had at various times with Ursula K. Le Guin, Naomi Shihab Nye, Evelyn C. White, Elizabeth Woody, and Teresa Jordan about how and why to go public with personal material. I also had useful conversations with Barbara Wilson about the nature of memoir.

I want to thank my students, particularly those on whom I tried out early versions of these ideas: participants in "Writing the Memoir" at the Flight of the Mind and at Haystack in the summers of 1994, 1995, and 1996, and all the 29th Street Writers, past and present. The questions they raised, their enthusiasm for the memoir, and their marvelous responses to my writing exercises, were all instrumental in the creation of this book.

Thanks, too, to Eighth Mountain Press interns Lila Lee, Susanna Rankin-Bohme, and Tricia Kenealy for research and Kathy Hyzy for indexing.

I was inspired by many memoirists, and in particular by Paul Monette (1945–1995), whose writing taught me much about the power of the truth.

And finally, to the best editor anyone could hope to have, Ruth Gundle of the Eighth Mountain Press, I extend great gratitude and appreciation for her unwavering commitment to making books that are intelligent, beautiful, and as useful in the world as they can possibly be.

Introduction

On March 4th, 1920, Virginia Woolf attended the first meeting of the Memoir Club, a group convened by Molly McCarthy. There were about a dozen of them—all old friends and members of what we now call the Bloomsbury Group—and one of their stated goals was "absolute frankness." At that first meeting, two women, McCarthy and Woolf's sister, Vanessa, and three men including Vanessa's husband, Clive Bell, read autobiographical essays aloud to the assembled company. At the second meeting, Woolf read "22 Hyde Park Gate," a shockingly revealing memoir about her half brother George Duckworth's incestuous relationship with her and her sister (published much later in *Moments of Being*). She reported in her diary that the experience left her "most unpleasantly discomfited." "I couldn't help figuring," she wrote, "a kind of uncomfortable boredom on the part of the males, to whose genial cheerful sense my revelations were at once mawkish and distasteful. What possessed me to lay bare my soul!"

Now, with a reading audience hungry for personal stories, memoirs are appearing in ever greater numbers. But laying bare the soul with absolute frankness is still an act of courage for women and for men too, though for somewhat different reasons. Men, even today, are not supposed to be preoccupied with soul searching: to be honest about their inner lives and their relationships is still uncomfortably close to transgressing the male role. For women, deeply personal writing can also be described as a rebellion against the expected role, though in the case of women, the expectation is that we *will* be preoccupied with inner lives, with relationships, and with family, but that we will gear our stories to satisfy, flatter, or collude with our immediate circle. In spite of twentieth-century inroads, men are still pushed to be actors and women caretakers. Neither role fits very well with making art out of truth.

As soon as I started to write about my own life, I understood that to speak honestly about family and community is to step way out of line, to risk accusations of betrayal, and to shoulder the burden of being the one who blows the whistle on the myths that families and communities create to protect themselves from painful truths. This threat was like a great shadow lurking at the corner of my vision, as it is for anyone who approaches this task, even before the writing leads them into sticky territory.

I was moulded into a pursuer of truth by my times. Active in the early feminist movement and shaped by the consciousness-raising that insisted on scrupulously examined lives, I was challenged in my twenties to take a second look, and then a third and fourth one, at the facts of my life. I was inspired by pioneers like Woolf and, over the years, cherished the increasing number of memoirs written by a wide range of women—women of color and white women, heterosexual women and lesbians—and also by men of color and gay men. I was able to witness how the social movements we created, movements whose members had previously been marginalized or invisible in literature, brought about radical changes in both our determination to tell our stories and in our access to publishing. This flowering of voices paved the way for more and more people to tell their stories, whether or not they participated in these movements, and whether or not they felt personally impacted by social change.

My own route to memoir was via poetry. Although the rhythms and images of poems were often what led me into the stories I wanted to tell, more and more I found myself needing the expansiveness of prose to explore them further, even after I had shaped them into verse. Since I couldn't always remember the facts surrounding an event, I found myself making up certain details and embellishing the story whose essence demanded that I give it form. For a while I was confused about this: did it mean I ought to be writing fiction? How much could I really make up? Could I trust my memory at all? What were the rules of memoir anyway?

I could find little to help me as I considered these questions. Once in a while I would have a conversation with a writer friend about truth and memory; occasionally I would debate the boundaries of fiction and memoir with a fiction writer. I read as many memoirs as I could get my hands on, noticing the memoir's surprising ability to adapt its form in the hands of different authors and in the service of varying subjects. I puzzled over its relationship to the more formal essays I had learned to write in school and wondered whether I should be polishing up those old techniques or trying to forget them.

This book, then, is the kind of book I once looked for but was never able to find. It opens up the conversations about memoir I wish I'd had when I was starting out and addresses the nuts-and-bolts questions that pertain to the memoir genre, as well as some others that apply more generally to prose writing. Having now taught the memoir for several years, I also offer a few linguistic and grammatical definitions that many of my students who are excellent writers missed out on along the way.

I hope this book will encourage all of you who are drawn to tell your own stories, for I think this is very important work.

For members of marginalized groups, speaking personally and truthfully about our lives plays a small part in erasing years of invisibility and interpretation by others. And for all of us, engaging seriously with the truth challenges our society's enormous untruthfulness—whether it comes from the family, which so often denies its own violence behind closed doors, or from the national and international powers that deny their own violence and call it "peace-keeping."

To write honestly about our lives requires that we work at and refine our artistic skills so that our memoirs can effectively communicate the hard-won, deep layers of truth that are rarely part of conventional social discourse. It requires, too, that we grapple with all the ethical questions that arise when we shun commonly accepted definitions of loyalty: questions like "can I really tell that story or will it hurt my mother?" By demanding our "loyalty" in the form of silence, some of the people we are closest to have coerced us into collaborating with their lies. We cannot, however, respond to this coercion by rushing angrily into print. We must examine our responsibility as writers to those we write about, even while holding fast to our truths.

In this book, I assume that the reader aspires to the highest literary standards, and I provide tools that I hope will be helpful to the serious creative writer. However, I trust it may also encourage and assist the many who are not yet, or may never be, thinking in terms of publication.

Finally, a word about pronouns. I started writing this book with both the memoir writer and the reader referred to as "he or she," but soon became hopelessly entangled in my own verbiage. Next I tried alternating. Sometimes the writer was "he" and sometimes "she," with the reader switching back and forth similarly. With this method it often became unclear whether I was referring back to the writer or to the reader. Finally, I adopted the present system, in which the writer is always "she" and the reader always "he." I beg both male writers and female readers to forgive me if they should momentarily feel excluded from these generic pronouns. The shortcomings of any gender-neutral system that I can currently think of are less the shortcomings of the splendid English language than of those whose biased usage has created a difficulty we have yet to solve.

It is my hope that this book not only will encourage you to dig down into your deepest layers of understanding but will also provide useful tools for the crafting and shaping of the truths you find there.

1

What Is Memoir?

When I was young, famous men—usually retired generals, Shakespearean actors, or the disillusioned relatives of such people—wrote "their memoirs." I never read them but imagined them to be the boring ramblings of old fogies puffing themselves up. "So-and-so is writing his memoirs" was a phrase I might have heard occasionally. "So what?" would be my unspoken response as I turned back to my favorite reading: long, exciting novels with complicated plots and a cast of characters that required concentration.

Like many people today, I confused "the memoir" with "memoirs." It was easy to do back then, when the literary memoir was not basking in the popularity it currently enjoys. The term *memoirs* was used to describe something closer to autobiography than the essaylike literary memoir. These famous-person memoirs rarely stuck to one theme or selected out one aspect of a life to explore in depth, as the memoir does. More often, "memoirs" (always preceded by a possessive pronoun: "my memoirs,""his memoirs") were a kind of scrapbook in which pieces of a life were pasted. Of course, the boundary between these genres was not—and still is not—as clearly delineated as

I have made it sound. Sometimes a book will be subtitled "a memoir" when it would seem really to belong more appropriately under the heading of memoirs or autobiography. Ned Rorem's *Knowing When to Stop: A Memoir*—which contains excerpts from journals and a variety of styles that, however fluent and interesting, do not form a shapely whole— is an example of such a book.

In my early reading days the memoir was in short supply. Looking back, I see that certain writers were paving the way for the contemporary literary memoir—Virginia Woolf, for instance, laid the groundwork for the frankly personal writing that would later become widespread. At the time, however, the library seemed to offer only fiction or essay. Essays were hard work, and I grumbled when, at twelve or thirteen, my English teachers made me read authors such as Charles Lamb and William Hazlitt. Now that I am writing my own stories, I have come to realize that the modern memoir belongs to the same family as those essays. Phillip Lopate, in his illuminating writings about the essay, includes the memoir (along with rumination, anecdote, diatribe, scholarship, fantasy, and moral philosophy) under the general heading of "the informal or familiar essay." It is not any particular form, he says, that distinguishes this kind of essay, but the author's voice.

The great essayist Montaigne understood "that, in an essay, the track of a person's thoughts struggling to achieve some understanding of a problem *is* the plot, is the adventure." Rather than simply telling a story from her life, the memoirist both tells the story and muses upon it, trying to unravel what it means in the light of her current knowledge. (One place where this musing voice was not possible was in the African-American slave narratives that nevertheless form a part of the modern American memoir's history. Trying to appear "objective"— to narrate simply the facts of her life without interpretation or judgment—the author of a slave narrative was all too aware of potential accusations of being inflammatory or of exaggerating the facts of the story.) The contemporary memoir includes retrospection as an essential part of the story. Your reader has to be willing to be both entertained by the story itself and interested in how you now, looking back on it, understand it.

In order for the reader to care about what you make of your life, there has to be an engaging voice in the writing—a voice that captures a personality. In all kinds of informal essays, including the memoir, the voice is conversational. One modern relative of the informal essayist is the newspaper columnist, whose chatty style is immediately recognizable in contrast to the impersonal, expository style of the formal essay or of the journalism found elsewhere in the newspaper. Memoir, like column writing, requires that the reader feel *spoken to*. In ear-

VOICE

Barbara Drake, writing about poetry says: "*Voice* is the medium and instrument of poetry, whether that poetry is spoken aloud or read silently. Voice is also the mark of the individual poet." This definition is also true for prose writing. We tend to think of voice as being something we hear; it can be squeaky or mellow, loud or soft. But in writing, voice is what we hear in our head: the medium.

A writer's voice is usually considered to be developed when it becomes recognizable. This may seem odd, given that the writer will sometimes assume the persona of another character or another aspect of herself. The fiction writer may speak through many very different characters, yet voice is something like the fingerprint of the writer—not the persona on the page but the writer with her own particular linguistic quirks, sentence rhythms, and recurring images. The memoirist needs to have this fingerprint too, even if she only speaks as herself.

lier days, this conversational quality included direct address from the writer to the reader ("Gentle reader..."), but this faded from view after the heyday of the memoir in the mid-nineteenth century. Still, even without the direct address, modern memoirs aim to speak intimately to their readers, and those readers like to experience them as if they were sitting in a comfortable chair listening to a series of confidences.

Although the roots of the memoir lie in the realm of personal essay, the modern literary memoir also has many of the characteristics of fiction. Moving both backward and forward in time, re-creating believable dialogue, switching back and forth between scene and summary, and controlling the pace and tension of the story, the memoirist keeps her reader engaged by being an adept storyteller. So, memoir is really a kind of hybrid form with elements of both fiction and essay, in which the author's voice, musing conversationally on a true story, is all important.

Sometimes when I teach the memoir, a student will ask: "But how is the memoir different from autobiography?" Certainly some memoirs are booklength and therefore contain as much material as many autobiographies. But a memoir is different, and the difference has to do with the choice of subject matter.

An autobiography is the story of a life: the name implies that the writer will somehow attempt to capture all the essential elements of that life. A writer's autobiography, for example, is not expected to deal merely with the author's growth and career as a writer but also with the facts and emotions connected to family life, education, relationships, sexuality, travels, and inner struggles of all kinds. An autobiography is sometimes limited by dates (as in *Under My Skin: Volume One of My Autobiography to 1949* by Doris Lessing), but not obviously by theme.

Memoir, on the other hand, makes no pretense of replicating a whole life. Indeed, one of the important skills of memoir writing is the selection of the theme or themes that will bind the work together. Thus we discover, on setting out to read Patricia Hampl's *Virgin Time*, that her chosen theme is the Catholicism she grew up with and her later struggle to find a place for it in her adult spiritual life. With a theme such as this laid down, the author resists the temptation to digress into stories that have no immediate bearing on the subject, and indeed Hampl's book tells nothing about many other aspects of her life, although it abounds in good stories. Vivian Gornick's memoir *Fierce Attachments* sets as its theme the story of the author's relationship with her mother. By setting

---

FIRST PERSON

(Because so many of you never had this in school.)

When we say something is written "in first person," we mean "first person singular." We mean that the narrator uses "I."

First person (singular)	I	I woke up this morning.
Second person (singular)	You	You woke up this morning.
Third person (singular)	He/she/it	He woke up this morning.
		Susan woke up this morning.
		The cat woke up this morning.
First Person (plural)	We	We woke up this morning.
Second person (plural)	You	All of you woke up this morning.
Third person (plural)	They	They woke up this morning.
		Susan and Jill woke up.
		The whole family, including the cat, woke up this morning.

boundaries, the writer can keep the focus on one aspect of a life and offer the reader an in-depth exploration.

When you select the material for a memoir, you will be keeping other material for later. Most people only ever write one autobiography, but you may write many memoirs over time. Mary Clearman Blew compares this process with the making of a quilt:

> *Remember that you have all colors to choose from; and while choosing one color means forgoing others, remind yourself that your coffee can of pieces will fill again. There will be another quilt at the back of your mind while you are piecing, quilting, and binding this one, which perhaps you will give to one of your daughters....*

Another way of looking at the difference between memoir and autobiography is expressed by Gore Vidal in his memoir *Palimpsest*. "A memoir is how one remembers one's own life," he says, "while an autobiography is history, requiring research, dates, facts double-checked." Although some memoirs do, in fact, call for research, the verifiable facts are not generally as important as they are in autobiography, where the author includes much that is beyond the realm of memory.

A word here about travel writing, which is an example of how fluid are the boundaries we have put around various types of writing. While often discussed as a separate genre, travel writing often overlaps with memoir. Sybille Bedford's *A Visit to Don Otavio: A Traveller's Tale from Mexico* is just one example of how nonfiction writing that gives information about a place can also accommodate the personal travel story that reads like memoir. Alice Adams's stories of Mexico have some of the same qualities.

Not every author of true stories chooses to label her work memoir, even if it has many characteristics of that genre. *Dwellings* by Linda Hogan and *Never in a Hurry* by Naomi Shihab

Nye both contain stories that could be called memoirs. Nye's book is subtitled "Essays on People and Places," locating the book in the larger category of personal essay, though the writings abound with the kind of stories we often think of as memoir. Hogan's collection is subtitled, rather more mysteriously as far as genre is concerned, "A Spiritual History of the Living World," but the jacket copy tells us that this is a work of non-

THE NARRATOR

The narrator is the protagonist of your memoir. It's a term also used in fiction and poetry, and refers to whomever is telling the story.

When thinking about your memoir or discussing it with your writing group (if you have one), you should always refer to the character who is you in the story as "the narrator," not as "I." Similarly, your friends or colleagues should refer to the protagonist of your story as "the narrator" and not as "you."

Although you are both the writer of the memoir and the central character of the story, they should be treated as two distinct entities. Thus, a friend could appropriately ask: "why did you [the writer] describe the *narrator* [protagonist] as a mouse on page three?" (Not: "Why did you describe *yourself* as a mouse on page three?")

Separating *yourself as writer* from *yourself as protagonist* will help give you the necessary perspective to craft the memoir as a story. It will also decrease the degree to which you feel exposed as others critique your work. (The information you reveal about yourself is the same no matter what terminology is used, but it can be less uncomfortable to hear others speak of "the narrator's" intimate experience than of "your" intimate experience.)

fiction, and the personal storytelling certainly hints at memoir.

Students often struggle to define the boundary between memoir and autobiography, or memoir and travel writing, and sometimes wonder which personal essays are memoirs, but they rarely ask about the difference between memoir and fiction, perhaps because it seems obvious that one is true and the other made up. But the more I think about memoir, and thus about truth, the less obvious—and the more important—that distinction becomes. After all, not everything in a memoir is true: who can remember the exact dialogue that took place at breakfast forty years ago? And if you can make up dialogue, change the name and hair color of a character to protect the privacy of the living, or even—as some memoirists do—reorder events to make the story work better, how is that different from fiction?

In memoir, the author stands behind her story saying to the world: this happened; this is true. What is important about this assertion is that it has an *effect on the reader*—he reads it believing it to be a true story, which in turn requires the writer to be an unflinchingly reliable narrator. In fiction, a story may be skillfully designed to sound like a true story told in the first person by a fictional character (who may be a quite unreliable narrator), but if the writer presents it as fiction, the reader will usually perceive it as fiction. Readers tend to look for, even to assume, the autobiographical in fiction, but they also recognize the writer's attempt to fictionalize, just as they recognize in memoir the central commitment *not to fictionalize*.

In this way, when you name what you write memoir or fiction, you enter into a contract with the reader. You say "this is true," or you say "this is imaginary." And if you are going to honor that contract, your raw material as a memoirist can only be what you have actually experienced. It is up to you to decide how imaginatively you transform the known facts— exactly how far you allow yourself to go to fill in the memory gaps. But whatever you decide about that, you must remain limited by your experience, unless you turn to fiction, in which you can, of course, embrace people, places, and events you have never personally known. While imagination certainly plays a role in both kinds of writing, the application of it in memoir is *circumscribed by the facts*, while in fiction it is *circumscribed by what the reader will believe*. These very different stages for the imagination allow recognizably different plays to be acted out on them.

You may interpret this contract with the reader differently from other writers, perhaps feeling freer to tamper with the details or choosing to invent more of the dialogue. Some memoirists, like Fern Kupfer in *Before and After Zachariah*, conflate several characters into one composite character and acknowledge in the book what they have done. Others reorder events into a different chronology or, like Deborah Tall in *The Island of the White Cow*, compress several years into one. (For some reason, I feel freer to mess with time than with people.) But although there is room for disagreement about many of these choices, you will gain little of value if you end up abusing the reader's trust. Making up a "better ending" to your story, while presenting it as true, or, worse still, inventing a whole piece of your life because it makes a good memoir, will often backfire. Readers may initially believe you if your deceptions are clever, but the more successful you are as a writer, the more likely it is that you will eventually be caught. Lillian Hellman's acclaimed "memoir," *Pentimento,* (later made into the film *Julia*) caught the public's imagination and was highly acclaimed, but later turned out to be more or less untrue: Hellman had never even met the real-life Julia. Had she lived to produce more memoirs, her disillusioned readers would have been less willing to place their trust in her words. In any case, her reputation undoubtedly suffered.

Even if no one ever finds out that you tampered with the facts, your memoir will suffer if you are dishonest. It is very difficult to be both candid and deceptive at the same time, and a memoir does need to be candid. Tampering with the truth will lead you to writing a bit too carefully—which in turn will rob your style of the ease that goes with honesty. Dishonest writing is very often mediocre writing. Especially when written in the first person, purporting to be true, it has a faint odor of prevarication about it. It's the kind of writing that leaves some of its readers with a nagging doubt: *What exactly was it I didn't believe?*

Of course, none of this should prevent you from speculating about the facts. Readers easily recognize the honesty of your desire to make sense of whatever few facts you may have. Musing on what *might* have been behind that old photograph of your grandmother, or telling the reader how you've always *imagined* your parents' early lives, is not the same as presenting your speculations as facts.

One last characteristic of the memoir that is important to recognize is one which also applies to essays, and which Georg Lukacs described as "the process of judging." This may seem problematic to some aspiring writers, since so many of us have been influenced, through various therapeutic or self-help philosophies, to believe that judgment is bad. We connect it with "judgmental," often used nowadays as a derogatory word. But the kind of judgment necessary to the good personal essay, or to the memoir, is not that nasty tendency to oversimplify and dismiss other people out of hand but rather the willingness to form and express complex opinions, both positive and negative.

If the charm of memoir is that we, the readers, see the author struggling to understand her past, then we must also see the author trying out opinions she may later shoot down, only to try out others as she takes a position about the meaning of her story. The memoirist need not necessarily know what she thinks about her subject but she must be trying to find out; she may never arrive at a definitive verdict, but she must be willing to share her intellectual and emotional quest for answers.

Without this attempt to make a judgment, the voice lacks interest, the stories, becalmed in the doldrums of neutrality, become neither fiction nor memoir, and the reader loses respect for the writer who claims the privilege of being the hero in her own story without meeting her responsibility to pursue meaning. Self-revelation without analysis or understanding becomes merely an embarrassment to both reader and writer.

o o o

When you sit down to begin working on a memoir:

First, remind yourself that you are not writing your autobiography: You do not have to write your entire life. So begin thinking in terms of theme and focus.

Second, get into an opinionated, or at least questioning, frame of mind.

Third, go to the library and check out a few good memoirs to read.

And finally, above all, remember that it's essential to *find your voice*. You can begin practicing right away.

❶ Think of a family story you have told or have heard told many times. Make notes about it and decide what the *theme* of the story is. Then write the story down succinctly. Do not stray from the theme and do not explain who the people in the story are. Do not give background information.

❷ Imagine you are talking to a close and trusted friend. Write down your thoughts about the story from #1 above as if talking it over with that friend, assuming she has already heard the story. Do you think it is true as told? What was left out so that everyone could feel comfortable with its being a family story? What does it say about the people involved and what does it say about you?

❸ Write the whole story again incorporating some of the speculations from #2 or letting some of the insights from #2 change the way you tell it.

❹ Pick a few other well-known personal stories (don't write the stories; just name them: "the story about the time when…" etc.). For each one, write down "I used to think this story was about … [fill in], but now I think it's really about… [fill in]."

❺ Make a list of your family's (or other close-knit group's) classic stories—those that are often repeated. For each one, make notes on what purpose you think it serves, or what myths it fosters in the family or group.

❻ Make a list of ways you could focus a memoir, starting with certain defined periods of time, such as "The year I went to college," or "first grade," or "the year my mother died."

❼ Make a list of themes you could use to focus a memoir, such as your relationship to food, sex, a sibling, your work, your dog, houses you have lived in, etc.

❽ Pick a particular person—a close friend, trusted family member, interested teacher or mentor—and imagine telling her or him all about one of the topics generated in #6 or #7. Write down what you confide, including actually addressing the person by name. Notice, as you read through what you've written, whenever the writing does not use the kind of words you would use if you were actually talking. Revise it to make it sound more like a spoken conversation.

2

Who Cares? and Other Thoughts on Getting Started

Many of us," writes Natalia Rachel Singer, "have gotten one too many 'who cares?' written in red ink on our work." The real question for anyone writing from his or her own life, she goes on to point out, is "why do *you* care about this?" But it can take a long time for the memoirist to get to that second question. The red ink, the echoes of "nobody could possibly be interested in *my* life," and the implications of self-indulgence raised by that persistent "who cares?", all combine to crush self-expression. One of your first tasks, then, is to ask yourself: why do I care about this? The answer will make you feel entitled to tell your own story—to accept that it is not only worthy of being written down but fit material for literature—something you want to revise and craft until it is beautiful. In time you will even come to believe that your story is important for other people to read.

Singer also points out that women and people of color, in particular, have felt the brunt of the "who cares?" syndrome. Memoirists from all backgrounds may find it hard to believe that their own lives are suitable subjects, but the authoritative voice required for writing memoir can be particularly elusive for those traditionally denied authority in the world, those more accustomed to being the objects than the subjects of literature. Speaking with authority for some feels both unfamiliar and dangerously presumptuous.

Nancy Mairs describes her particular struggle. Just beginning work on the material that ended up as *Remembering the Bone House*, she took some written sketches of houses she had lived in at different times to a workshop taught by "a well-known southwestern writer of nonfiction." This writer told her that her memoirs were not readable, but added: "If you were already a famous person this might not matter." Initially stopped by this devastating criticism, Mairs responded logically: "I hadn't any chance of becoming a famous person. No fame, no life. I put the copy book with its blotchy black-and-white cardboard covers away." Later, being both smart and persistent, Mairs began to question whether fame was an authentic requirement for writing memoirs and returned to the work to produce one of the most moving and beautifully crafted memoirs of our time.

The sad part of such stories is that these discouraging messages so often come from teachers or mentors—people we look to for encouragement and validation. For this reason, it is essential to pick your teachers carefully. If you want help in starting to write memoirs, you don't want to fall into the clutches of a famous writer who has been hired to teach at a writing workshop solely because of his name's ability to attract students, rather than because of any teaching skill. You should not have to grapple with someone who secretly thinks you should be writing about *his* life rather than your own.

But making the right choice is not always easy. Reading potential teachers' published work can give you some insights into their attitudes, but even (or especially) if they are really good on the page, you can sometimes be badly surprised in the classroom. Asking around among previous students can also be useful, but beware the "star-struck" mentality that afflicts some students of unscrupulous teachers, particularly those few students chosen by the famous writer for encouragement at the expense of the others in the class. Naturally, the select few will speak well of such a teacher, but the teacher you are looking for will be equally generous to all his students. I advise very thorough research. There are good, supportive, honest teachers out there. There are also egomaniacs.

◦ ◦ ◦

Whether you are a beginning writer setting out to learn about the memoir or an experienced writer turning from poetry or fiction to this new form, it is important to remember that it takes time to learn. Writers, more than most other artists, seem to expect of themselves instant expertise. Perhaps this is because we all use words in everyday life, whereas we don't all use violins or oil paints. With other art forms, it is more obvious that there must be a long apprenticeship.

We writers see this attitude—the belief that writing is as easy as getting out of bed—expressed all around us. Bill Roorbach, writing on apprenticeship, records comments from nonwriters similar to ones most of us have heard. There was the couple who, hearing that Roorbach had published a memoir about traveling with the woman who later became his wife, told him, "We could have written that book.... Always wanted to take off a month and write the darn thing." And the doctor at a cocktail party who told him she was going to take six months off and write *her* story. Roorbach's satisfying comeback was, "You know, you've inspired *me!* I'm going to take six months off and become a surgeon!" The point, of course, is not to put down people who are ignorant about the time it takes to become a writer but to establish, in the face of a denial that can seriously undermine our learning process, the fact that a long apprenticeship is needed in literature as in any other field that requires the acquisition of skills.

APPRENTICE

Apprentice (from the French *apprendre:* to learn): One bound by legal agreement to serve another for a certain time with a view to learning an art or trade in consideration of instruction and, formerly, of maintenance; hence a beginner; tyro; novice.
(Webster's Collegiate Dictionary)

Today, the would-be writer must patch together an apprenticeship. If you are serious about the craft, your learning may be helped along by various writing teachers through writing programs or workshops, or sometimes through less formal meetings or correspondence. If you are very lucky, you may find one teacher to see you through all or part of a long apprenticeship, but more likely you will work with several teachers, as well as peer groups that offer support and critique. But remember that extensive reading is probably the most important ingredient of your apprenticeship, whether or not you have a teacher. You will never become a good writer if you urgently want to write but do not have an equal passion for reading.

Most successful writers today no longer live the lives that those in earlier times enjoyed, when they were able to take young writers under their wings, read their early efforts, correspond with them, and generally help them through their apprenticeships. Nowadays, almost all literary writers work long hours, often at things other than their writing, and struggle to find time for their creative work. Many writers do serve as mentors through classes or workshops, or by offering critique of manuscripts for pay. In these circumstances, when you set out to find a mentor you should exercise restraint. *Do not* approach a writer with four hundred typescript pages under your arm (or even four), with a view to getting a free critique. If you want the expertise of a successful writer, you should offer to pay for his or her time.

I once heard the poet Olga Broumas say that it takes at least ten years for someone to become a poet. A similar statement could be made about becoming a memoir writer. During that ten years (or however long it takes for you to feel that you can move beyond apprenticeship), strangers or acquaintances will ask what you do. If you tell them you are a writer, as Roorbach points out, they will almost certainly ask what you have published. Better to say you are an apprentice writer, which has a lot more dignity than an unpublished writer in the eyes of the world, where to be an unpublished writer is to be either a dilettante or a failure. People who never think about these things seem to assume that a real writer is born with a book already on the best-seller list.

In fact, writing memoir takes not only apprenticeship in the craft itself but the constant gathering of suitable themes, incubation time, and the musing on your material that will bring insight to the final story—a preparatory period that is needed for all kinds of creative writing. Susan Griffin describes it as a difficult time during which she fears "that there is no intrinsic authority to my own words." "I...clean off my desk," she says. "I make telephone calls. I know I am avoiding the typewriter. I know that in my mind, where there might be words, there is simply a blankness. I may try to write and then my words bore me." But when the time *is* right, the waiting will have been worth it. "Because each time I write, each time the authentic words break through, I am changed. The older order that I was collapses and dies. I lose control. I do not know exactly what words will appear on the page. I follow language. I follow the sound of the words, and I am surprised and transformed by what I record."

❧ ❧ ❧

Once you are comfortable with the idea of being an apprentice and have put aside thoughts of agents, publishers, audience, fame, or fortune—none of which is conducive to good writing—it is time to think about what it is that you really care about.

In deciding what to focus on, you can find important clues by examining your preoccupations: What things do you think about over and over? What stories haunt you? Which people from the past do you dream about? What makes you passionate when you think about it or talk about it? What do you argue about? Most of us have ongoing obsessions, sometimes as a result of difficult, tragic, magical, or unexpected events or circumstances in our lives. Sometimes these are the things we studiously avoid writing about, but sooner or later we come to realize they are our bedrock material. The fact is that writing, like any creative undertaking, carries with it both pain and great joy. The pain is often inherent in the most fertile subject matter; the joy lies in transforming that subject matter and thus moving through it in a way that helps us grow while we create something of value to others.

If you have already begun a few memoirs and find yourself feeling impatient with them as you read and reread them, chances are they are not pushing you to a place of deep exploration. Or you are stopping short of the deeper truths that you both want and don't want to uncover. In this way, writing mimics life: you have to be willing to take enormous risks to reap enormous rewards.

As you get started, it will be important for you to keep a notebook in which you write down random ideas, images from dreams, snatches of conversations from the past, and anything else that comes into your mind that hints at a memoir waiting to be written. It always seems odd to me that a story can stay buried in my memory for years and years, but the minute it surfaces into consciousness as a story idea, it is likely to get lost. If I don't grab it as it begins to form itself as a narrative, it can become permanently erased, and even if I remember the general subject matter, the voice that started narrating in my mind eludes me. It is a good idea to have a notebook small enough to carry with you and to keep one beside your bed. In the middle of the night you will be convinced that your great idea will wait for you until morning, but, sadly, a great many fine stories have been lost with the ring of the alarm clock. You can become adept at recording the important phrase or image that will later take you back to that moment of insight when you glimpsed the story. For some, it's the opening sentence that leaps to mind; for others, a shadowy shape of the whole thing, or maybe even the heart of the story. Whatever it is for you, write something in your notebook that will bring it back when you have time to explore it.

Some books on writing life stories offer long lists of subjects to jump-start you. They include things like the arrival of a sibling, your first day at school, career choices, getting married, and so on, but these can often lead to wooden writing that bypasses the heart of the matter. It is not the obvious landmarks of a life that hold the passionate moments, the transformations, and the painful growth: those lie within incidents and relationships that are unique to each of us. So rather than taking off from such a list, create your own list. Find that haunting story that has nothing to do with what looks like one of life's "big moments." Use your notebook to search diligently among your lifelong preoccupations.

You may, at this early stage, find yourself struggling to stay with the writing. You may be looking for any excuse to get up from your desk. At this point I suggest you do the "blocks exercise," listed under "Suggestions for Writing" at the end of this chapter, and spend some time validating your difficulties and fears. Beware, though: it is easy to spend all your available writing time thinking or even writing about *not writing*—some writing groups, for example, talk endlessly about their difficulties but never actually write anything. So do not go overboard. Use the blocks exercise to take a good hard look at what gets in your way, write about it, and then move on.

As you get going, it is important, too, to go to other peoples' memoirs for inspiration. Although there are an astonishing number of aspiring writers who seem to be uninterested in other people's books, you simply cannot be a good writer unless you are also a good reader. Just as composers go to concerts and artists visit galleries, writers read. You will learn, in the most enjoyable way, more about style and language from reading good literature than you will ever acquire from workshops and how-to books. Reading other peoples' memoirs will give you concrete ideas about how to organize your own stories and demonstrate just how many different approaches you can take.

Other peoples' memoirs, too, will remind you of how much you can care about someone else's experience when it is written well. It is useful to keep a list of memoirs that have moved you so you can go back to them when you want to check out how they did that. For me, one such memoir is *Road Song*, Natalie Kusz's engrossing story of life in Alaska and the terrible accident that so badly disfigured her face. Reading her book, I was absolutely engaged with her particular challenge, even though it was very far from any experience of my own. For the time it took me to move from front cover to back, her difficulties became mine; her environment—though I had never been to Alaska—became home. From time to time I was reminded of something in my own life that, though quite different, had called up a similar response to Kusz's, but often I simply left my own experience and shared hers. Later, when struggling to believe that my own story could possibly matter to unknown readers, the fact that I had read and identified with Kusz's story helped me. Although the memoir I was working on was about the difficulty I had had in grieving for my parents, who drowned when I was nineteen—certainly not an experience shared by most potential readers—I realized that, if I did it well, some of those readers could have that same experience of identification that I valued so much. Moments in my life might resonate with moments in theirs. They might even step right outside their familiar histories and share mine for a while.

Whenever a story allows you to enter it in this way, remember that it is because the writer herself has grappled with the events she is recounting and has passionate thoughts about their consequences in her own life. Which brings us back to the importance of caring. Part of why *you* care, of course, is because you can tell how much *she* cares. So start thinking right away about what matters in your own life—what has most challenged you, formed you, influenced you. Start making lists and notes. And from time to time remind yourself who cares: *You do.*

❶ This is what I call the "blocks exercise." It has several different parts to it. Don't read ahead, but do each section in turn. If necessary, cover the page below as you go along. If you do this with a writing group, have one person read the instructions for one section at a time, including the time allowed for writing, and keep to the time limits for each part.

➤ First, make a long list of everything you can think of that gets in the way of your writing. Think of things that fall under the headings of both "external" (taking care of children, cleaning the house, spending eight hours a day at work, etc.) and "internal" ("I've nothing new to say"; "my life's not interesting"; "people will be shocked," etc.). Keep adding to the list even after you think it's done. (5 minutes)

➤ Read through the list and check the item that has the most power over you. It may be a different one next week, but follow your instinct for *today*. (2 minutes)

➤ Imagine you are talking to a trusted friend. Write a two- or three-page description, in first person, of a *particular* time when you grappled with this problem. Be specific: Where were you? What thoughts did you have? Don't generalize to other times. (25 minutes)

➤ Now go back and read through the story you've just written and turn it from first person into third person.

Substitute a name that is not your own for the first "I" and change the pronouns to he or she, altering verbs to fit. Don't rewrite the whole thing—just be prepared to be messy! (5 minutes)

➤ Finally, read aloud (or silently if you are in a group) the story in its new third-person form. When you have listened to yourself read it, make some notes on the following or discuss with your group. (20 minutes)

How do you feel about the narrator? Are you sympathetic to her, or are you impatient? What advice would you give her? (There are no right answers.)

Do you have a different relationship to the subject you chose when it is written in first and third persons? If so, write yourself a reminder that you can always, in the future, get some distance from your material—particularly when generating painful stories—by switching to third person.

Do verb tenses also have this power? Try out a passage in both present and past tense. Use the same story if you like and see if the present tense brings you and your reader closer to the subject matter. (See Chapter 6 for a discussion of the pitfalls of narrating in present tense.)

❷ Write about someone from the past who made you feel that your life or your stories were important.

❸ Write about someone from the past who made you feel that your life or your stories were *not* important.

❹ Write about someone whose story or life provided inspiration or encouragement to you.

❺ Write about the process of learning something over a period of time and what that felt like at different stages until you mastered it.

❻ Make a list of topics about which you feel passionate. What do you argue about? Think about? Want to change? What things happened in your life that "changed everything?" What stories do you hurry to tell a new friend or lover? Which stories that haunt you do you not want to tell?

3

Finding Form

D o not make the mistake of thinking it is easier to tell the stories you have lived than to make up fictitious stories about imaginary people. It is no easier to write your own story well than it is to write anything else well. Like any other literary genre, memoir requires you, as Annie Dillard has said, "to fashion a text." An important part of this crafting is finding the right form for your story—a structure that is more than simply an adequate vehicle for the facts. The form must actively enhance the subject matter, subtly reveal layers of meaning, and complement the shape of the story with its own pleasing structure.

Form in memoir varies widely. As Barbara Wilson—a long-time fiction writer who is also the author of a memoir—has observed, memoirs at this time seem much more different from one another than do novels. Some memoirs, like those of Paul Monette in *Last Watch of the Night,* are closely related to the essay, while others, like Esmeralda Santiago's book-length *When I Was Puerto Rican*, employ fictional techniques and read much like novels or short stories.

Nancy Mairs, in *Remembering the Bone House,* describes the

form of her book as "the fragmented form of essays, each concentrating on a house or houses important to my growth as a woman." Although the whole book tells a story, each essay works as a separate piece, contributing to the whole in a way that is less integrated than, say, a chapter of a conventionally structured novel, where the plot develops sequentially.

Lucy Grealy's *Autobiography of a Face* is also organized by theme, and is made up of twelve pieces with titles like "Petting Zoo" and "Truth and Beauty," many of which stand alone, although, like Mairs's essays, together they tell a whole story. Because each piece focuses on a thematic aspect of the overall topic (Grealy's struggle with cancer of her jaw), the book is not always chronological. Overall, the reader moves through the experience with Grealy, but within each chapter we may follow a particular theme through a span of time that, whether long or very short, overlaps with the time covered by other chapters on different themes.

In *Fierce Attachments* by Vivian Gornick, exact dates are unimportant. In this book, some scenes take place in the present or recent past, where the narrator and her mother are walking the streets of New York talking, and others are set in the more distant past, which is often what the two are talking about. Although the book jumps back and forth in time, Gornick helps the reader to differentiate between different eras by narrating in the present tense for one and past tense for another. Chronology, in her book, is suggested and understated, unlike some memoirs that carefully date every scene. Richard Hoffman's *Half the House*, for example, is divided into chapters each headed by a date from 1956 to 1990, although they are not always in exact chronological order.

Gretel Ehrlich's *A Match to the Heart* is subtitled *One Woman's Story of Being Struck by Lightning*, which sets us up to read it as a memoir—which it is. Yet Erlich's own story is interspersed with sections that are more like essays on the nature of lightning. First we get the personal, highly physical, description:

*The inside of my eyelids turned gold and I could see the dark out-
lines of things through them. At the bottom of the hill I opened
the door to my pickup and blew the horn with the idea that someone might hear me. No one came. My head had swollen to an
indelicate shape. I tried to swallow—I was so thirsty—but the
muscles in my throat were still paralyzed and I wondered when
I would no longer be able to breathe.*

Then the book moves from the close-up to the big picture.
Here, scientific facts abound and could easily disrupt the flow
of such a personal story, yet the often-poetic voice of the author
pulls it all together, reminding us that this speaker, who is telling us more than we ever thought we'd know about the origin
of storms, has been personally assaulted by the scientific phe-
nomena she is describing:

*A thundercloud grows unruly, as all cities do, when the shear-
ing stresses between ascending and descending air—as with the
wealthy and the poor—result in turbulence. In addition, when
dense dry air from outside the cloud is displaced by the updraft,
it mixes with saturated air, thus providing a constant supply of
recently warmed air full of moisture. This is fed to the upwardly
mobile tower. Once begun, the cloud builds on itself, sometimes
rising 40,000 feet in the air.*

*All summer these stately empires sail above Wyoming moun-
tains, processions of cool heads, but inside they are dynamic, cha-
otic districts drawn into existence by jets of buoyant air, growing
in volume and height until they bump into the upper reaches of
the stratosphere. Even then, they sometimes continue upward,
their turrets penetrating stable layers of air until they can go no
further, then they fall back on themselves.*

If you are writing about a particular time or place and have
set your boundaries clearly around the period or location, one
way you could structure your memoir is to focus on different

people in turn as Teresa Jordan did in *Riding the White Horse Home*. Set in Wyoming, the memoir is about the four generations of her family who ranched on Iron Mountain. The place itself dictates the boundaries, demanding that all the stories add something to the underlying theme—the family ranch, now lost to the author, and western ranch life, now nearly extinct. Some chapters like "How Coyote Sent the White Girl Home" relate the author's own memories, while others like "Marie," about the author's great-aunt, focus on other people: family members, neighbors, people who worked on the ranch. Of course, Jordan is not absent from these portraits, since her own relationship with the people concerned informs what is remembered or, in some cases, researched, but the focus shifts from character to character as each chapter builds the narrative.

These are just a few examples of the many different forms a memoir can take. You can check out the ways they are organized simply by picking up examples from your library shelf. You might read Lucy Grealy's book with an eye to how carefully she picks her themes, or Esmeralda Santiago's with attention to her use of scene and dialogue. In fact, any well-written memoir is worth perusing with an eye to its structure.

❧ ❧ ❧

Sometimes the form may seem to you like a container for the story—say, a pot. Of course you want the most beautiful pot you can make, as well as one that is the right size and shape for what it is to hold. However, you can't just go and choose a pot from a pot store. Rather, you must make your own vessel as your material begins to take shape; you must work with it, mould it as the story expands, and let it swell where it wants to, or taper down to a fine mouth when necessary.

Other times, the form may seem to come from the inside—more like a skeleton or a tree trunk. When you find that sturdy trunk and some of the main branches, then the foliage shapes itself naturally around the skeleton.

Sometimes clues about form emerge as your material begins to shape itself: the words may start to fall into a pattern or follow a rhythm, and if you allow poetic language into your prose, the sounds of the words themselves may help you arrive at an appropriate form. If you stay alert to this aspect of your output, you will most likely get a glimpse of the form just when you begin to need it: a shape will appear that suggests the beginnings of a structure: something indefinable that you know is the right vehicle for exploring your story even further.

If you have a vision of the form early on, or perhaps even before you begin, be open to the idea that though it may seem like the perfect one, it may also be simply what gets you started. You must be willing to adapt it, revise it, tinker with it, or entirely rethink it, later in the process. If, however, you initially have no clue as to the form you need, then you must rely on blind faith that sooner or later it will appear. You may need and enjoy the freedom of relative formlessness for a while—but not forever.

Some memoirs have begun as letters to the authors' children, as extended journals, collections of photographs, or as poems. I started "Poetry and Prejudice," a seventeen-page memoir, as a narrative poem—one which grew longer and longer, but never satisfied my need to speculate about the events it describes. The leap into prose finally allowed me to expand the retrospective voice and turn it into memoir (although some of the poetry, particularly a repeated phrase that functioned as a refrain, remained in the final version). Use whatever works for you to start gathering together your memories, but don't mistake that method for the final form. You have a lot of work cut out for you between the journal page and the final draft of your memoir.

❧ ❧ ❧

In Chapter 1, I said that a memoir is not an autobiography but rather a selected aspect of a life. How you select that aspect is crucial to the success of your piece. You have to know—not necessarily right away, but at some point—what it is that you really want to write about, which in turn will tell you what to leave out. If you're not careful, all kinds of extraneous details, or even unnecessary plot lines, will insinuate themselves into your good graces until, before you know it, you have a huge chunk of autobiography sprawling across your screen or notebook.

Plot—what actually happens in your story—is an artificial construct. Life doesn't have a shapely plot in the way that fiction often does. Instead, it goes on day by day with an ever-shifting focus as various themes unravel over time. As you shape your memoir, you will need to select events from this random package in order to bring an element of plot into the picture.

Being willing to leave things out is vital. One way to think about this is to understand that, for you, all your memories are connected: they are all part of your life, and as such they form a whole. This means that you might set out to write a memoir about, say, your father, and you may need to describe the restaurant where the two of you often ate together, which of course is connected to the neighbor who also liked to eat at that restaurant, who later became a good friend of your father's. As you plough into the neighbor's history, your memoirist's antennae should start trembling. The neighbor's story is connected to you and your father both in real life and in your memory, but is it—should it be—connected in the pages of your memoir? It may be frustrating for you to say no to that piece of what seems to you like a whole. You may feel you are shortchanging the complexity of your story. Yet, for your story to resonate on deeper levels, it will require careful pruning. Annie Dillard recalls having to leave out a vacation in Wyoming because, although important in her life, it did not directly relate to the theme of *An American Childhood*.

At the beginning of Stephen Spender's *World Within World*, the author speculates about the form of his book. Most of the events, he tells us, occur between 1928 and 1939. "Outside this decade," he explains, "I have chosen only material which concerns my own story, and I do not attempt to fill in the background of the time."

Pay attention to those words: *I do not attempt to fill in the background*. Your memoir will assume enormous proportions and quite possibly leave your readers confused or exasperated if you give the entire historical context. Although you will want to bring aspects of the wider world into your story, you have to know where to draw the line. It is inevitable that you, as both the writer and the subject of the story, will know far more than you can tell. For the memoir to work, you will always have to lop off a piece of a bigger story.

❧ ❧ ❧

Although in this book I will frequently urge you to dig deep for the heart of your stories, this does not mean they have to be long stories. Some of you may stop yourselves from writing by worrying about the right length, but there is no right length for the memoir, though there probably is for *your* memoir. Memoirs can be any length, from one or two pages to large books. In Denise Levertov's collection, *Tesserae: Memories & Suppositions*, for example, there are many very short memoirs, some of which are primarily portraits of people or places from the past, infused with the speculations of the adult looking back.

"The Gardener" in this collection describes "old Day," who worked for the author's parents and their neighbors when she was a child. Old Day was both ornery and a little frightening to the child, but at the end of the very short memoir the author, as an adult, hears one of those now elderly former neighbors assert that old Day can't possible still be alive. She responds:

> But I know better. Bone and mist, pale, white-haired, grey-eyed, very tall, clothed in colors of ash and earth, a capricious demi-god, he still moves in a stately shamble up and down the block, glides unobserved right through certain houses, brings life and blossom, death and burial to the rectangular sanctums closed off from each other by walls of brick and thickets of may, laburnum, apple trees, memory, time. He carries sometimes a spade, sometimes a scythe, and listens in silence to orders he will not obey. He has his own intentions.

In a remarkably short piece of writing, Levertov gives us the two very different perspectives—that of the child and that of the adult—which are such a necessary characteristic of memoir.

You may not know when you start on your memoir whether it will be two pages or two hundred. The pace, the degree of expansiveness, and the potential scope of the subject will all become apparent as you work your way in. When I started to generate the material that eventually became my memoir, *Lifesaving*, I thought I was writing a few short memoirs. It didn't occur to me until I had generated well over a hundred pages that they wanted to get together and become a book. In retrospect, I'm glad I didn't know this when I began; sometimes, with certain subjects at least, we need a degree of ignorance in order to plunge in.

❧ ❧ ❧

I struggled hard to make a shapely whole out of the pile of stories that would eventually become *Lifesaving*. These stories recounted my life in a small Spanish town where I lived in the early sixties. I had moved there at the age of nineteen to work as a tour guide and interpreter for a winery shortly after my parents had drowned in a cruise ship disaster. I knew that my reaction to my parents' deaths had to be central to the book, which ostensibly told a rather different story. The grief and loneliness that underlay my adventures needed a form in which to emerge as an unexpressed but real part of the experience.

Then one night, just when I was becoming quite frustrated with the difficulty of the task, I dreamed what I thought was an additional story—a story about the lifesaving classes I had taken as a child. In the morning I wrote out the dream as a new chapter, though it seemed quite out of place among the other pieces, whose subject matter and time period were so different. Suddenly, it occurred to me to break up this new piece and insert small italicized sections of it *between* all the other stories. Where this idea came from seemed somewhat mysterious at the time, but later I saw that I had probably been helped by having recently read *The Great Deep: The Sea and Its Thresholds* by James Hamilton-Paterson, a book with a similar kind of structure—yet another reminder of how our reading is always there to help us.

As I cut the "lifesaving" section into short pieces of a few sentences each and placed them between stories, I was astonished to find that several of them related directly to the stories they followed or preceded. By leaving out a paragraph here and there, and by doing considerable reordering, I was able to add the whole lifesaving section in a way that not only linked the stories but also articulated the speculations and obsessions that accompany the grief of any survivor of a disaster. With this added material, the stories worked on deeper and deeper levels. I still had work to do, but the dream had been a crucial turning point. My book had found its form.

❶ Write a very short (not more than two pages) memoir about someone outside your family from your childhood. Include your perspective both as a child and as who you are now.

❷ Select a theme for a longer memoir—a potent theme that runs through your life (food; travel; your relationships with animals; a phobia; etc.) and write the opening two pages. Read through what you have written and jot down some ideas for how to link the different episodes you might add, how to divide the piece, whether it will be chronologically arranged or follow some other pattern, and other thoughts about possible forms.

❸ Focus on your relationship with one family member or long-term friend and:

> ➤ Make a list of stories connected to that person (the trip you took together to...; the argument over...; the time when...; etc.).

> ➤ Make a chronological list of dates when significant things happened to you and that person.

> ➤ Draw a line like a graph showing the "ups and downs" of the relationship over time, with notes on the peaks and valleys denoting times of closeness, fun, difficulties, etc.

➤ Decide how you would organize a short memoir about this relationship.

➤ Decide how you would organize a long memoir about this relationship.

4

The Truth:
What, Why,
and How?

Those of us who write memoirs find ourselves speculating frequently about truth. What is it? How can one person know it? What is its relationship to facts? As Mary Clearman Blew has written: "For my part, I struggled for a long time with the conflicting claims of the exact truth of the story and its emotional truth as I perceived it."

Although both factual truth and emotional truth are important in memoir, sometimes, as Blew said, the two are not the same. If you do too much research, you may find that the story you have carried around in your memory for twenty years can't be true after all because the dates don't match up or someone left before someone else arrived. Personally, I hate research, which may be why I like to write memoirs, for which I rely primarily on memory.

Not all memoirists are like me, however. Some do extensive research prior to writing their story. Ian Frazier spent two and a half years researching things as diverse as American Protestant culture and the making of angel food cake before embarking on his memoir, *Family*. Eileen Simpson studied masses of correspondence, including more than six hundred of her own letters to her sister, before writing *Poets in Their Youth*.

If, however, like me, you find research a bore, you should still be prepared to check certain facts. I am now resigned to having to research some things to make my memoirs accurate. It can be embarrassing to get some very public fact wrong: the date Kennedy was shot; who played in the final at Wimbledon that year; or—one that I almost failed to catch before it went into print—whether you're going southeast or southwest when driving from Barcelona to Gibraltar. If these matters of public record figure in your story and you get them wrong, you will get dozens of letters telling you how sloppy your work is. On the other hand, only a handful of people will bother to tell you that Aunt Miriam got pregnant before that summer vacation in Maine, not after.

Matters of public record aside, though, try not to worry about someone else recalling your story differently than you do. Remember William Stafford's advice on writing good literature of any kind: "The research for what you are writing is your whole life—I mean, there is one world expert on it: you.... For what you're writing there is no other authority."

When writing memoir, I sometimes reorder events to make the story work. I approximate dialogue that I can't recall word for word. I frequently leave out whatever makes the story too complicated for a stranger to grasp. At the same time, while taking these liberties with factual truth, I feel honor bound to capture the essence of the interaction in the events as I order them and in the dialogue as I re-create it. Memoir is, after all, supposed to be a true story; you have a certain obligation to the reader to make it that.

But are the facts always the same as the truth? Toni Morrison doesn't think so. "The crucial distinction for me," she says, "is not the difference between fact and fiction, but the distinction between fact and truth." Perhaps, as memoirists, we have to make our peace with the possibility that there is no more an absolute truth in memoir than there is in life. Anna

Akhmatova said that every attempt to produce a memoir amounts to falsification. Perhaps our task, then, is to decide where, in each story, the integrity—the honest heart of the story—rests, while at the same time giving due respect to the events as we remember them.

A word of warning here. The events as you remember them will never be the same in your memory once you have turned them into a memoir. For years I have worried that if I turn all of my life into literature, I won't have any real life left—just stories about it. And it is a realistic concern: it does happen like that. I am no longer sure I remember how it felt to be twenty and living in Spain after my parents died; my book about it stands now between me and my own memories. When I try to think about that time, what comes to mind most readily is what I wrote. And I have no idea if that is more or less true than the original memories.

๑ ๑ ๑

One thing we can probably agree on is that the truth, however we define it, is often hard to tell. It can be hard to tell the facts of the story, and it can be hard to tell its emotional truth too. First there's the pain we can cause ourselves in private through the very act of getting close enough to the truth to write it down. Then there are all the fears that go with publication: self-revelation, physical or emotional retaliation, loss of a job, loss of privacy, causing embarrassment, causing distress, social ostracism, and losing friends or family, are just some of the consequences we face—or believe we face—when we consider speaking out about something we suspect people want us to keep quiet about.

Sometimes these fears are the result of clearly verbalized threats: "You can't write about *that*—it will kill your mother," or, "You'll never be welcome in my house again if you tell that story." We are often told that keeping quiet is a kind of loyalty, that speaking out is a betrayal of family, colleagues, friends, institutions, country. No one has to tell us these things. We just *know*. We know in advance about the raised eyebrows, the turned backs, the gossip. We know what is expected of us and what we must do to be approved of. Women, especially, know that we are expected to keep the peace, smooth over conflict, unpleasantness, and unhappiness, and always "make nice."

Virginia Woolf understood this requirement for women when she wrote "Professions for Women" in 1931, which even now doesn't sound particularly outdated. Woolf describes the phantom she had to battle in order to tell the truth and express her own honest opinions. She names that phantom "the Angel in the House":

> *I will describe her as shortly as I can. She was intensely sympathetic. She was immensely charming. She was utterly unselfish. She excelled in the difficult arts of family life. She sacrificed herself daily. If there was chicken, she took the leg; if there was a draught she sat in it—in short she was so constituted that she never had a mind or a wish of her own, but preferred to sympathize always with the minds and wishes of others.... And when I came to write I encountered her with the very first words. The shadow of her wings fell on my page; I heard the rustling of her skirts in the room.*

Although Woolf's solution may sound extreme to us, perhaps extreme situations call for extreme solutions:

> *I turned upon her and caught her by the throat. I did my best to kill her. My excuse, if I were to be had up in a court of law, would be that I acted in self-defence. Had I not killed her she would have killed me. She would have plucked the heart out of my writing.*

Kathleen Norris, writing much more recently in her memoir *Dakota*, describes how in small, rural western towns, people often revise the history of those places by writing it down the way they *wish* it had been, rather than how it really *was*. They take care that the written record doesn't offend the descendants of pioneer families, and they edit out violence and hardship in favor of a more romantic version of the past. This attitude, says Norris, spreads into the present too: "If we can make the past harmonious, why not the present? Why risk discussion that might cause unpleasantness?"

Most people belong to some group that demands their loyalty. Telling the truth almost always breaks unspoken laws, the solidarity expected from members of that group, whether it be a family or a larger community. When Alice Walker published *The Color Purple*, which was fiction, not memoir, but which contained unflinching and believable depictions of violence by black men toward black women, Walker's loyalty to the black community was questioned and she was publicly attacked. In a recent memoir focused on the making of the film from that book, Walker writes, "It was said that I hated men, black men in particular; that my work was injurious to black male and female relationships; that my ideas of equality and tolerance were harmful, even destructive to the black community."

☙ ☙ ☙

Writing a memoir constantly raises Norris's question: Why risk unpleasantness? The fact is that "unpleasantness" of various kinds can follow not only your deliberate revelations—the ones you expect to cause repercussions, such as family secrets involving abuse, *your* version of a failed relationship, or what actually happened to your friend who disappeared—but it can also be triggered by relatively innocuous tales. Even a joyful story can irritate someone who saw it differently. If you have siblings you probably already know that each of you has your own version of your shared past. Who was the favorite child? Why did your father leave? There may be as many answers as there are children in the family. No matter what story you tell, there can always be someone who didn't want to be mentioned, someone who ought to have been mentioned, or someone who thinks you got it all wrong.

So why, indeed, risk causing unpleasantness? You probably know the answer already if you are seriously engaging with memoir. For some reason particular to you and your life, you *need* to tell the truth. However, even if your own need is the driving force, it may be helpful, when you hit a rough spot, to remember that other people, too, need you to tell the truth. Sometimes those who most need you to speak out are those very people who plead with you to keep the family secrets hidden.

Remember, too, the readers you will never meet who will one day write and thank you for your honesty. Most of us can name one or two books we have read that changed our lives. These books often had their impact because they said something we had never heard said before, or because they treated a subject of great importance to us in a way that helped us think about it, and eventually talk or write about it ourselves. It is those truths, whether or not they mirror our own experience, that sustain us and our culture.

We all learn from one another's stories, which is, perhaps, the great gift of memoir. At its best, a memoir offers not only a well-written piece of prose but also a story we know is the writer's actual experience. Indeed, it is what Fern Kupfer calls "the authority of the truth" that makes the memoir so attractive to us. We watch the memoirist make sense of her life and no matter how different our circumstances, we find some commonality with her and feel a little less alone in the world. This sense of shared humanity is a very important aspect of culture. Memoirs, in that they are stories we believe to be true, offer a direct entry into this sharing, even while their authors, in all their diversity, demonstrate how differently people may look at the world.

You may find yourself doubting that large numbers of readers will be able to relate to your particular story. Why should someone quite different from you want to read about your childhood? Alice Walker, in *The Same River Twice*, addresses this (referring to Theologian Howard Thurman):

> He said that if you go deeply enough into yourself, into your own idiom, it's inevitable, then, that you come up in other people. We have the capability to connect to absolutely everyone and everything, and, in fact, we are all connected.... When I write about my family, about things from the South, the people of China say, "Why, this is very Chinese."

◦ ◦ ◦

Although you may be convinced about the need for truth, you may encounter some subject matter that feels so prohibited that it has become taboo. Overcoming your own inhibitions is only the first step in dealing with these monsters. They also present particular difficulties for the tone and style of the writing itself. Most taboo subjects are painful ones: childhood abuse, sexual violence, alcoholism, certain mental and physical illnesses—the list is long and recognizable. The subjects are difficult not only for you, the writer, but also for the reader, whether or not he has actually experienced similar things. Although your story may be a valuable gift to your readers, it may also be something they are reluctant to get close to. Therefore, you must ask yourself how to write in a way that is engaging without compromising the truth.

Some writers use humor. This is a wonderful way to engage the reader, and is also very hard to pull off when the subject is a somber one. A good example of the powerful merging of serious truth with humor is "Oranges and Sweet Sister Boy" by Judy Ruiz, which begins, "I am sleeping, hard, when the telephone rings. It's my brother and he's calling to say that he

TABOO

Taboo, tabu: n. 1. A prohibition excluding something from use, approach, or mention because of its sacred and inviolable nature. 2. A ban attached to something by social custom. *(The American Heritage Dictionary of the English Language)*

The Oxford Universal Dictionary gives additional characteristics of taboo: Taboo, tabu: adj. As originally used in Polynesia, Melanesia, New Zealand, etc.: Set apart for or consecrated to a special use or purpose; restricted to the use of a god, a king, priests, or chiefs, while forbidden to general use; prohibited to a particular class (especially to women), or to a particular person or persons....

When struggling with writing "difficult" material, it might help us to remember the origins of the word *taboo*. The first form of the word was *tabu*, which was the Tongan word for "sacred." If we consider the most difficult, most taboo subjects to be sacred subjects, then perhaps we will be encouraged in the important work of telling our truths—including those that have been banned "by social custom" or "forbidden to general use."

is now my sister." The memoir deals not only with the author's brother's sex-change operation but also with her own institutionalization as a paranoid schizophrenic at the age of eighteen. These are not light subjects, yet, without sparing the reader any of the horrors of the mental hospital or of her brother's pain, Ruiz manages to inject a tone of wry humor frequently enough to prevent the piece from getting bogged down. For example, when she refers to the sex-change as "the Blade question," we know she is not going to be too earnest:

News can make a person stupid. It can make you think you can do something. So I ask the Blade question, thinking that if he hasn't had the operation yet that I can fly to him, rent a cabin out on Puget Sound. That we can talk. That I can get him to touch base with reality.

"Begin with an orange," I would tell him.

Whether or not you employ humor in dealing with difficult subjects, the *tone* of the writing is of the utmost importance. Personally, I can read about almost any subject if I feel a basic trust in, and respect for, the writer. The voice must have authority. But more than that, I must know that the writer is all right. If she describes a suicide attempt or a babysitter's cruelty to her, or a time of acute loneliness, I need to feel that the writer takes full responsibility for her experience. The tone may be serious, ironic, angry, sad, or almost anything except whiny. There must be no hidden plea for help—no subtle seeking of sympathy. The writer must have done her work, made her peace with the facts, and be telling the story for the story's sake. Although the writing may incidentally turn out to be another step in her recovery, that must not be her visible

TONE

Tone is a changeable aspect of voice. While the voice is always that of the author in question, the tone may be angry one day, ironic another. The tone is an indication of the writer's attitude toward what she is writing about. It is often created in part by word choices. In the opening section of Patricia Hampl's memoir, for example, (see page 124) the choice of the words *lingo* and *fiefdoms* are instrumental in creating the tone.

motivation. Her first allegiance must be to the telling of the story and I, as the reader, must feel that I'm in the hands of a competent writer who needs nothing from me except my attention.

I must also feel confident that I'm not being used by the writer to get revenge on one of the characters in the story. If her desire to humiliate an "enemy" outweighs her commitment to a meaningful story, the tone will surely reflect her motivation, and she will lose me as a reader.

Difficult as it is to approach taboo subjects, do not be too quick to assume that your story will be heavy on trauma just because you remember the wounds so well, and because they perhaps moved you to write the story in the first place. Some people remember only the sad things about their childhoods but find, as Jill Ker Conway did when writing *The Road from Coorain*, that working on a memoir reawakens many happier memories that they may have forgotten.

ɞ ɞ ɞ

Telling your truths—the difficult ones and the joyful ones and all the ones between—is a big part of what makes for good writing. It is also what brings you pleasure in the *process* of writing. Most people who create and tend a garden don't spend time on their knees pulling weeds just for the perfect end result—the gorgeous display of flowers that others will exclaim over. They pore over gardening books, order bulbs, water a sickly shrub, arrange the flagstones to make a pleasing path, all because they enjoy the *doing* of it. So, too, it should be with your writing. You want to see your writing grow, to find your daily work absorbing, to discover you can do better on the page than you could three years ago. None of this will happen if you shy away from the truth. Your reader will see exactly what you have done and so will you. The rewards that you seek are the rewards that go with courage: you take the risk ("why risk causing unpleasantness?") and you feel the satisfaction of becoming a better writer.

I should say here that truth alone does not make for good writing. You may have read, as I have, some pieces of writing that are painfully truthful but nevertheless boring, embarrassing, or annoying. And you may have heard their authors, on hearing mild criticism, defend themselves with an indignant "but it's *the truth*," as if that alone guarantees literary excellence. If the writer is more interested in writing to humiliate someone from the past than in working her story into a form that transcends her desire for revenge, no amount of factual truth will save it. It is that unique blend of truth and art—a blend that may take years of practice to achieve—that can touch a reader's heart with immediate sorrow or lift a reader's spirits in a flash of recognition.

◦ ◦ ◦

Having encouraged you to engage with your personal history and with the truth however you see it, I now want to encourage you also to think about what you choose to put out in the world. The freedom of speech you enjoy means that you have choices and at some point you need to stop and consider why you choose to share the ideas, stories and words that you do.

I believe that as writers our purpose must be something more than a mere urge toward self-expression and must be fueled by something beyond a romantic view of the writer's life. When we tell our stories we are playing a part in shaping the culture. As poet Elizabeth Woody has said: "Our words make the world."

We all have different approaches to these choices: you, for instance, may believe it important to write the graphic details about the abuse you suffered as a child, naming the perpetrators, while I may choose to focus on the stories that precede and surround similar abuse. One writer may believe that stories of healing are the only ones worth writing at this time in history, while another may choose to make a painstaking record of the natural world. Some of us judge what is worthwhile by what makes people laugh or cry, others by what makes people think or what supports social change. What is most important is not that we agree but that we each think about what is valuable for us to contribute, and that we make conscious choices.

Toni Cade Bambara once wrote: "I can't get happy writing ugly weird. If I'm not laughing while I work, I conclude that I am not communicating nourishment, since laughter is the most surefire healant I know." Ursula K. Le Guin, when dealing with painful subjects, makes a distinction between "wallowing," which she says she writes but does not share publicly and "bearing witness," which she does share. Andrea Carlisle decides whether something is appropriate to make public by asking herself hard questions about the piece: "Am I asking something for myself—for the readers to feel sorry for me, for them to like me, or for them to feel as bad as I do—or is the work its own thing, asking nothing but to be heard and felt?"

None of these writers has the answer for you, but each is giving serious thought to her own participation in creating our culture. I encourage you to do likewise. Hold fast to your own truths, knowing that your freedom to tell them is accompanied by a responsibility to your readers that you cannot ignore.

❶ Think of an incident that one or more people might see very differently than you. Tell the story beginning with the words, "This is how I see what happened...."

❷ Kathleen Norris, in *Dakota*, has a chapter called "Can You Tell the Truth in a Small Town?" Think of a similar title, substituting for "a small town" another group such as "my family," "this neighborhood," "the hospital where I work," "the gay community," "an army camp," "the classroom," "Washington, D.C.," or others that occur to you. Write about the subject, making sure it stays personal.

❸ Make a list of everything you consider taboo for yourself. Think about which things on the list you could begin to write about.

❹ Write a memoir beginning with the words "It would be much too dangerous to talk about...."

❺ Tell the story (without any trivialization or modesty) of something in your life you are proud of.

❻ Write a graphic sex scene from your life. Be specific, physical, and clear. Try to avoid using metaphors or clichés.

5

*Scene,
Summary,
and
Musing*

When you write memoirs, you find yourself telling stories. Sometimes the whole memoir is one story interspersed with the narrator's commentary; sometimes the memoir focuses on a theme, illustrated by many different stories. However you structure the memoir, you will need to employ certain fiction-writing skills in order to make the most of the story element. Scene and summary are two important ways of moving through a story. What I call "musing" is an added element, sometimes present in fiction, but always essential to memoir. I have noticed that many beginning writers use summary to the exclusion of scene and dialogue, while writers who are experienced in other literary genres are often leery of musing, since they have been well drilled in the "show, don't tell" school.

One way of understanding scene and summary is to think of them in cinematic terms: the summary is the long shot—the one that pulls back to a great distance, embracing first the whole house, then the street, then the neighborhood, and then, becoming an aerial shot, it takes in the whole city and maybe the surrounding mountains too. This view can include a huge number of details, but all seen from a distance, none apparently more important than another.

The scene, on the other hand, is more like the close-up, the camera zooming in through the kitchen window, picking out the two figures talking at the table and going up really close to the face of first one speaker then the other while the audience hears each one speak. Many details of the kitchen are lost with this shot: maybe a blurry blue pitcher on a sideboard behind one of the speakers can just be discerned; perhaps there is a vague impression of yellow walls and an open door. But in this scene it is the speakers and what they say that matters. Only selected details are in sharp focus.

Translated into literary time, these two approaches represent different paces. We use the summary when we want to cover a lot of time in a few paragraphs; it gets us from the end of one scene to another scene a year later, and on the way there it fills in information that is important to the continuity of the story.

Scene, on the other hand, deals with a much shorter span of time; we slow down the narrative to something more like the actual time it takes for the scene to unravel in life. Because the writer is going in close and because there is no need to crunch a lot of time into a small space, she can give the exact dialogue, note the expressions, reactions, and movements of the speakers, as well as sounds, sights, smells, etc., in the immediate environment. She may go inside a character's head and give us thoughts that aren't expressed in the dialogue. She may describe in some detail the facial expression of one character. She selects which details to render in sharp focus.

As you begin to intersperse your summary with scenes, beware of relying too heavily on the scenes to provide all the interesting writing. Summary, too, can offer rich, sensory detail and is certainly not merely a way of moving time along between scenes. This excerpt from Esmeralda Santiago's *When I Was Puerto Rican* shows just how engaging summary can be:

I started school in the middle of hurricane season, and the world grew suddenly bigger, a vast place of other adults and children whose lives were similar, but whose shadings I couldn't really explore out of respect and dignidad. Dignidad was something you conferred on other people, and they, in turn, gave back to you. It meant you never swore at people, never showed anger in front of strangers, never stared, never stood too close to people you'd just met, never addressed people by the familiar tú until they gave you permission....

In school I volunteered to wipe down the blackboard, to sharpen pencils, to help distribute lined paper in which we could write our tortured alphabets with the mysterious tilde over the n to make ñ, the ü, the double consonants ll and rr with their strong sounds. I loved the neat rows of desks lined up one after the other, the pockmarked tops shiny in spots where the surface hadn't blistered, the thrill when I raised my desktop to find a large box underneath in which I kept my primer, sheets of paper, and the pencil stubs I guarded as if they were the finest writing instruments.

I walked home from school full of importance in my green and yellow uniform. It was my most prized possession, the only thing in our house that belonged to me alone, because neither Delsa nor Norma were old enough to go to school.

But school was also where I compared my family to others in the barrio. I learned there were children whose fathers were drunks, whose mothers were "bad," whose sisters had run away with travelling salesmen, whose brothers had landed in prison. I met children whose mothers walked the distance from their house to church on their knees in gratitude for prayers answered. Children whose fathers came home every day and played catch in the dusty front yard. Girls whose sisters taught them to embroider flowers on linen handkerchiefs. Boys whose brothers took them by the hand and helped them climb a tree. There were families in the barrio with running water inside their houses, electric bulbs shining down from every room, curtains on the windows, and printed linoleum on the floors.

This section, which goes on for another page or so, summarizes a large chunk of time, specified only as the time when the narrator "started school." When we read the verbs in the phrases "I walked home from school" or "I met children," we know that the speaker doesn't mean that she walked home from school on any one particular day, or that she met children only on the first day of school. Because this is summary rather than scene, the verbs refer to an ongoing set of actions that took place over time. Although this summary gives many interesting details and employs vivid images such as "the pockmarked tops shiny in spots," it never moves into a scene, which would require the writer to fix on one particular day within that period.

A scene will often begin with a specific time location such as "one day in spring," "Thursday afternoon," "three weeks' later," or "at five o'clock." Here is the beginning of another piece from Santiago's memoir. You can compare the specific time location, and the close-up style of the scene, with the summary in the previous example.

Sunday morning before breakfast Abuela handed me my piqué dress, washed and ironed.

"We're going to Mass," she said, pulling out a small white mantilla, *which I was to wear during the service.*

"Can we have breakfast first, Abuela. I'm hungry."

"No. We have to fast before church. Don't ask why. It's too complicated to explain."

I dressed and combed my hair, and she helped me pin the mantilla *to the top of my head.*

"All the way there and back," she said, "you should have nothing but good thoughts, because we're going to the house of God."

I'd never been to church and had never stopped to classify my thoughts into good ones and bad ones. But when she said that, I knew what she meant and also knew bad thoughts would be the only things on my mind all the way there and back.

Unlike the previous example, in this excerpt, because it is a scene, verbs such as "I dressed "and "combed my hair" refer to actions performed *once* on one particular day.

You will notice, too, that this scene, unlike the earlier summary, contains dialogue—that, in fact, the conversation between the narrator and Abuela plays a major role in pulling the reader up close to the action and bringing the two characters into sharp focus. To write good scenes you must grapple with dialogue, which requires not just that you listen carefully to how people actually speak, but that you select judiciously among all the things they say. Sometimes a student will protest, when her dialogue is criticized, "but that is exactly what they said," and I have no doubt that it's true. However, a transcript of real life does not make for an engaging story any more than a photograph taken from your window necessarily makes for a striking picture of your environment. In both cases, there are choices to be made: how close up the observer will stand; who or what will be in sharp focus; what will be left out; and many more questions of aesthetic significance, the answers to which will determine how pleasing or affecting the scene turns out to be.

As for making your dialogue realistic, there is no better test than to read it aloud as you write it and as you revise it again and again. Do not be tempted to add spice by way of the attributions. These are the "he saids" and "she saids," which you will sometimes need in order to make it clear who is saying what. Since the usual practice is to use a new line each time you switch speakers, attributions are likely to be needed less often than you think; use them only when the conversation would be unclear without them. Don't shore up the dialogue with descriptions such as "he snapped" or "she mused," or phrases such as, "he said in an endearing tone," or "she replied with a sarcastic edge to her voice." In the best writing, that kind of information is revealed in the dialogue itself and the reader gets to know the speakers through their own words.

In memoir, of course, you are writing true stories, and the re-creation of dialogue that actually occurred in your past raises again that sticky question of truth. You probably won't recall the exact words, except here and there when certain moments made a profound and lasting impact on you. Even if you can remember or if you have a record of a conversation, the faithful transcription of what was said is unlikely to work well on the page. You must select the best words, arrange the telling phrases, and move your story along with dialogue that adds to your depiction of the characters.

In most cases, you will not have a record and will have to improvise, always keeping in mind that you are not writing fiction. By all means, leave things out; by all means, make someone's speech clear, where it might have been so convoluted as to lose the reader; but work consistently toward the truth. For me, this again means looking hard for the heart of what actually happened, rather than for the good story that may have its seeds in experience but which takes off on a trajectory all its own.

❧ ❧ ❧

The "musing" element of memoir appears in two different forms. Sometimes it takes place right there on the page, visibly separated from the experience it is reflecting on; at other times the author lets us see that she has done her musing out of our sight but displays the resulting wisdom. What is always recognizable, though, is the presence of the retrospective voice.

An example of a memoir with a very clear-cut separation between the story and the retrospective wisdom is the poet James Merrill's *A Different Person*. Merrill tells the story of a thirty-month sojourn in Europe he took at the age of twenty-four. In each chapter, he tells stories from that time and then, at the end of the chapter, switches to a different voice, indicated by italics, to give the reader his current understanding of that chapter's events. He explains this at the end of the first chapter, when the italics first appear: "A different typeface for that person I became? He will break in at chapter's end with glimpses beyond my time frame."

This is a rather extreme example of a story in which the author's musings are separated out. Other writers may switch back and forth more frequently between story and musing with a less predictable separation, yet the separate elements will be apparent to the reader.

Sometimes, however, the retrospective voice is well buried within the narrative, as in Vivian Gornick's *Fierce Attachments*:

> *I lived in that tenement between the ages of six and twenty-one. There were twenty apartments, four to a floor, and all I remember is a building full of women. I hardly remember the men at all. They were everywhere, of course—husbands, fathers, brothers—but I remember only the women. And I remember them all crude like Mrs. Drucker or fierce like my mother. They never spoke as though they knew who they were, understood the bargain they had struck with life, but they often acted as though they knew. Shrewd, volatile, unlettered, they performed on a Dreiserian scale. There would be years of apparent calm, then suddenly an outbreak of panic and wildness: two or three lives scarred (perhaps ruined), and the turmoil would subside. Once again: sullen quiet, erotic torpor, the ordinariness of daily denial. And I—the girl growing in their midst, being made in their image—I absorbed them as I would chloroform on a cloth laid against my face. It has taken me thirty years to understand how much of them I understood.*

In this passage, the musing is woven into a summary section. The adult looks back at her childhood through the distance between now and then, and her current understanding is conveyed in phrases like "all I remember is..." and "It has taken me thirty years to understand...." She conveys what she has come to understand in quite subtle ways. For example, readers would know that this author has seriously speculated about the situation when they encounter the phrase "the ordinariness of daily denial." Here is the memoirist making a judgment (or expressing an opinion if you prefer) about how the people in her story maintained "apparent calm." Similarly, her description of the women reveals not only the women themselves but also her acquired insight into their lives and characters: "They never spoke as though they knew who they were, understood the bargain they had struck with life, but they often acted as though they knew."

You should watch out not to let the need for musing push you toward an earnest voice that appears to take itself altogether too seriously. While you must, in fact, take yourself very seriously in the memoir, the voice shouldn't be ponderous— it can be playful, ironic, humorous, or straightforwardly thoughtful. In *Stop-time,* Frank Conroy, for example, uses a tone that stops just short of poking fun at himself. There's a gentle humor about the voice he uses when he looks at the thirteen-year-old he once was:

> *Today nothing happens in a gas station. I'm eager to leave, to get where I'm going, and the station, like some huge paper cutout, or a Hollywood set, is simply a façade. But at thirteen, sitting with my back against the wall, it was a marvelous place to be. The delicious smell of gasoline, the cars coming and going, the free air hose, the half-heard voices buzzing in the background— these things hung musically in the air, filling me with a sense of well-being. In ten minutes my psyche would be topped up like the tanks of the automobiles.*

As noted earlier, the essence of memoir is "the track of a person's thoughts struggling to achieve some understanding of a problem." But can you really find the meaning of your story in the process of putting it down on paper, just as some people figure out the plot of a novel while writing? Will you know more about your life after writing your memoir than you did before you began, or should you have done all that unraveling beforehand? For most of us, there is a new level of understanding that comes along with the writing, but it's also true that we need to have done plenty of thinking about our lives before we start. Living a conscious and reflective life is a prerequisite for writing a memoir of substance.

This raises the question of how long it takes to be ready to write. As you read memoirs, you may notice that some people wait a very long time—twenty, thirty, fifty years—before they embark on the writing. Tove Ditlevsen's *Early Spring*, for example, was first published some forty years after some of the events it describes and demonstrates an extraordinary insight into childhood—one that clearly required many years of reflection before it could be written. Gretel Ehrlich's *A Match to the Heart*, however, deals with much more recent events, and focuses less on the layers of internal processing that happen over time than on the initial reaction to a traumatic event that is often externally focused. Each of these time frames works for the book concerned.

ꙮ ꙮ ꙮ

As you practice writing memoirs, you should try to notice where your strengths and weaknesses lie. Do you write pages of scenes, or perhaps spend most of your time musing? Although you will probably enjoy one or two of these aspects of the memoir best—usually the ones you do well—your memoir will be stronger if you make yourself work on those you are least drawn to.

Remember it is scene and summary that make for a good story, while musing in some form makes it layered and thought-provoking. All are necessary components of the memoir. No matter how wise you are about the events of your life, you must be able to turn those events into an engaging story. On the other hand, story alone cannot convey your memoir's deepest message.

At first as you look at these three elements, you can separate them out, giving yourself assignments in scene or summary, or writing a page or two of musing on a story you have already drafted. Thinking of summary as the long shot and the scene as the close-up, remind yourself that you are not merely one camera operator here, but that you are the director. You must deploy several cameras. You must call the shots, using all the approaches available to you.

Later, as your skills develop, the different elements will fall into place more naturally. Soon you will be able to trust that you are telling your stories using more than one approach. Even then, however, it pays to check back through your drafts, looking specifically for scene, summary, and musing. You will be able to do this better with the more dispassionate eye of revision than in that first heady rush of creation.

❶ Think of an event in your life when you were less than twelve years old. Write a straightforward narrative of the event in first person without musing or speculating on it.

❷ Read through the narrative created in #1 and think for a while about it. Try to decide what the story is *really about*— underneath the obvious facts. See if you can come up with an opening sentence that summarizes what it's about, such as: "When I was ten I learned something about loyalty," or "Parental inconsistency can drive you crazy," or "My last year in grade school I discovered death." Now write the story again using the adult voice of that first sentence. (You may later choose to discard the sentence.) Allow yourself to be *who you are now,* looking back at the event.

❸ Pick a summer from your early life and write an account of it all in summary.

❹ From that same summer, write two scenes.

❺ Write a memoir about mealtimes in your family (or another group you regularly ate with over a long period of time). Use scene, summary, and musing.

6

Moving Around in Time

There is more to writing a memoir than simply starting at the beginning and ending at the end. Sometimes, you may start at one point in time and go forward to another. Other times, however, the story may suddenly demand that you jump back twenty years and fill in some important facts. And what if you want to step out of the story and speak from the present time? What if the story takes place over many different time periods and you don't want to tell it chronologically? The reader needs to be able to follow your movement through time without really noticing it. One of the hardest things to do elegantly—and one of the things that requires the most solid understanding of how language works—is to move around in time without confusing your reader.

The first thing to remember is that there must be a "now." The reader must have a sense that the narrator is rooted in a particular moment from which he or she may look back, may speak in present tense, or may look forward to the future. The "now" doesn't have to be explicit. Readers don't care about the exact date, or even the decade; what they do care about is a sense that it exists and that it anchors a logical time span.

Often the narrator tells the story in past tense ("When I turned twelve I *went* to live with my father") and then goes further back in time, jumping over the past that's already been set up, using the past perfect tense ("Several years before I went to live with my father, *I had decided* I would have nothing more to do with him"). In this case, both tenses imply an unnamed present from which the speaker is looking back. Once established, that present time cannot move around.

Things get less flexible when the story is narrated in present tense. ("When I turn twelve, *I go* to live with my father.") It has recently become fashionable to tell stories in both fiction and memoir using the present tense to narrate the past (as has often been done in poetry). Some people claim that this method gives the story a kind of immediacy—that the reader feels more closely involved in the action. Others, like Lynne Sharon Schwartz, suggest that the present tense may sometimes function "to give the illusion of significance." However you perceive it, as Schwartz says, "When breaking with convention it is wise to know exactly why you are doing so, and what you may gain and lose, and whether you are simply substituting another convention with new and more disguised disadvantages." For someone just beginning to write, telling the story in present tense may cause difficulties that could be avoided by using the past tense.

One of the difficulties of narrating in present tense is, as Schwartz points out, that syntax and sentence structure are limited. This is partly because present-tense narration creates two different "nows." There is the "now" of the story itself ("The following year, *I go* to live with my father") and the implied "now" that is the time from which the story is actually being told. Grammatically, this second "now" doesn't exist. Yet the reader supplies it anyway, since he knows that events in the story are not literally happening as the narrator writes them down.

The two "nows" are not, by themselves, a problem, since

readers are smart enough to move between the two, even without the explicit direction of verb tenses. The problems arise when the writer wants to move to a different time period altogether—say, a much earlier time, or the actual present. Consider the options: "When I turn twelve, *I go* to live with my father. Several years before this, *I decide* to have nothing more to do with him." Or perhaps: "When I turn twelve, *I go* to live with my father. Several years before this, *I have decided* to have

VERB TENSES

There are three main divisions of time—present, past, and future. Various verb forms and verb phrases refer to divisions of actual time.

The four verb tenses mentioned in this discussion of moving around in time are:

PRESENT	I see; she walks
PAST	I saw; they talked
PRESENT PERFECT	I have seen; he has eaten
PAST PERFECT	I had seen; it had flown

nothing more to do with him." We need a way to indicate an earlier past than the past we are already in, yet neither option sounds quite right, perhaps because the present tense isn't really meant to recount the past. As you see, it gets murky.

And what about the actual present. Consider: "When I turn twelve, I go to live with my father. *I am* not sure of the wisdom of this, given our past histories." Here, it is unclear if the writer intends the second sentence, "I am not sure..." to be a musing statement made by the adult speaker in the actual present, or if it is just a continuation of the present-tense narrative from the twelve-year-old's perspective. By dispensing with the past tense, the writer has (grammatically at least) limited her expressive options.

In English, past-tense narrative is a little more straightforward than in languages that have a different verb tense to differentiate between onetime actions in the past and ongoing, frequent actions in the past. French, for example, uses the "imperfect" for ongoing actions in the past. While it may seem that the English options are simpler, our lack of an ongoing past tense means that we have to set up the passage in such a way as to make clear to the reader which kind of past action we are describing. This "setting-up" often involves a choice between scene and summary, with the summary representing the ongoing past—things that happened over and over again—and the scene depicting a onetime event in the past.

If you don't understand the mechanics of the language or fail to pay close attention to how your story is moving around in time, your reader will get lost. He will start turning back through the pages looking for clues. "Well, first the narrator was ten," he says to himself, still turning pages, "and then it was five years later. But what about this paragraph here that refers to when she was twenty-five?" These are questions *you* should be asking and answering while revising, sparing your reader any thoughts about the time frame.

ﻭ ﻭ ﻭ

I have sometimes found it useful to work with my students on diagramming the time span covered in a memoir. By paying attention to the clues given by different writers as they move from one time frame to another, you can see how both verb tenses and key phrases help the reader make those transitions. The following example of such a diagram uses some sections of "Poetry and Prejudice," a memoir of mine that covers a lot of different time periods. Here is the opening:

If only I had known what he was going to say when he stood up, I would have stopped him. But how? Don't read your poem out loud, Brad—you have no idea of the effect it will have on me? *Or, as I had said every other morning:* Please hand your papers up to me and I'll read a few of them aloud? *That had worked fine for the first four class meetings. I had been able to screen out the worst of the blood and gore. I had read the hunting poems, with their slitting of throats, removal of scalps, antlers, ears, and eyes, and their dragging out of guts. But I hadn't read the poems in which the throats being slit were human. As a criterion for selection I have some doubts about this now, but I had to think on my feet those mornings, leafing through a sheaf of unappetizing poems.*

I was the poet-in-residence at Enterprise High School, in the shadow of Oregon's Wallowa Mountains near the Idaho border. This first-period class consisted of twelve seniors—and I didn't like them. Unlike all the classes I had worked with the previous week, this one had not responded to any of my attempts to interest them in poetry. With only one more day, I had begun to think it wasn't going to happen. This frustrated me. Always before I had managed to make a good connection with my students.

Earlier that morning, I had driven, as I did every day before school, down the road from my borrowed cabin on Wallowa Lake toward Joseph, where I had worked several times as a visiting poet. I loved this part of the state. In fact, it had become one of those rare, special places where I could relax into the beauty of the landscape and work on my own writing in the quiet hours after school—one of those places that imprints its colors and its contours on my mind forever. Each time I had completed a residency here, I'd angled for return invitations, which, so far, had always been forthcoming.

As I approached the Indian burial ground, I turned for a last look at snow-covered Chief Joseph Mountain....

This excerpt, told in various past tenses, implies a "now" from which the narrator is speaking. This "now," can be marked with an X on the line which represents time. It is not actually specified what year or month "now" is, although it is referred to directly at the end of the first paragraph ("I have some doubts about this *now*"). All readers can know from this is that the "now" is somewhere on the line *after the time being described* in the story.

```
                                    NOW
Past                                 X                    Future
```

Once you have established the "now" with an X, you can look for the earlier time frames described in the excerpt. "Every other morning" in the fourth line, as well as "Earlier that morning" at the beginning of the third paragraph, both indicate that there is a particular morning in question. You can mark it on the time line as "that morning."

In the first paragraph you learn that something had "worked fine for the first four class meetings" and in the second that there was "only one more day." So "that day" can also be placed at the end of a particular school week.

Further, you learn in the second paragraph that the narrator had spent" the previous week" at the school, although not with this particular class. So "the previous week" is another piece of the past that can be located on the time line.

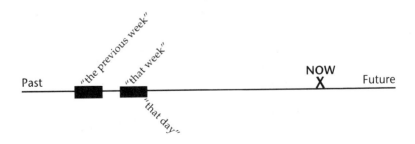

Finally, a further past exists in this excerpt, as indicated by the reference to the town of Joseph "where I had worked several times as a visiting poet" and by "Each time I had completed a residency here, I'd angled for return invitations...." Here, using the past perfect ("I had worked"), the narrator leaps over the past that has already been set up to reach a more distant past, which can also appear on the time line as "previous residencies as visiting poet."

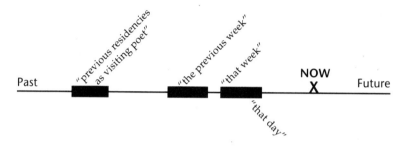

The memoir goes on to focus for several pages on "that day," telling the story of what happened in that particular classroom. Then, after a visual break on the page, a new time frame is introduced:

I moved to Portland, Oregon, from London almost twenty years ago. Although Portland is a fairly cosmopolitan city, my first few years in the West were marked by an enormous sense of culture gap. It took a long time to stop feeling foreign, even though I picked up the vocabulary and the accent much too fast for the comfort of my family back in England....

Who knows how long it would have taken me to put down real roots here if I had continued taking hikes and car trips, stopping at cafés that made home-baked pies, and chatting with the owners of small-town stores, many of whom eyed me with suspicion? It was the Arts in Education program that allowed me to go out and live in my adopted state, instead of cruising through it, a perpetual tourist.

I started with a six-week stint up the Columbia River in Hermiston, where I learned a lot about potatoes, irrigation, and the amazing number and diversity of churches that could thrive in a small community...

In this section, the narrator is still rooted in the same "now." But the time line extends much further back in time—to be precise, to "almost twenty years ago." Now you can make the original time line much longer, noting that nothing in this section must conflict with or confuse the earlier time frame.

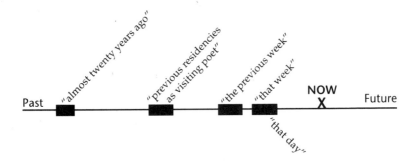

Having entered the precise time "almost twenty years ago," you can guess at where to enter the time referred to in the sentence "I started with a six-week stint up the Columbia River...." It must come after "twenty years ago," but considerably before the two weeks pinpointed in the first section of the memoir.

After this middle section, the memoir returns to the original story with the words, "Right after Brad read his poem that day...." By now, the reader knows what day "that day" is, and goes right back to the town of Joseph with the narrator.

The story continues through "that day" into the following morning and then, at the very end, jumps forward in time. The second-to-last paragraph begins with the words, "A few days after returning to Portland that spring, I put together a set of informational articles...." Since the story is still being narrated in the past tense, the reader knows that the narrator is still looking back from the "now." What is being described in the last two paragraphs is a piece of time somewhere between "that day" and "now."

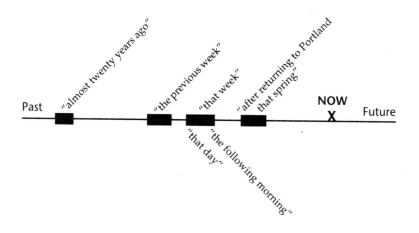

My advice is to practice jumping back and forth without losing your reader (or yourself). You will become so well versed with the extraordinary possibilities of the language that soon you will be able to do it elegantly and without hesitation. The time line is a device that can help you learn this skill by helping you see whether a piece of writing moves clearly from one time frame to another. Once you become adept at moving back and forth through time on the page, you won't need to think about it and nor will the reader.

❶ Find two or three short memoirs (short-story length as opposed to book length) and, for each one, create a time line. As you make the time line, list in your notebook the words or phrases the author uses to pinpoint a particular time, whether it be a specific day or an identifiable span of time. (Phrases such as "Later that day," "When I moved to Philadelphia," "My second year in college," or "Long before that summer," and so on.)

Good places to find short memoirs are collections such as *Modern American Memoirs* edited by Annie Dillard and Cort Conley and the annual *Best American Essays* series. Many quality literary magazines include memoirs.

❷ Tell the story of one particular vacation, narrating it in the present tense.

❸ Now rewrite the story in #2 in the past tense. Let yourself change the story if changes suggest themselves. Note what works best in each tense.

❹ Describe a job you have held or a kind of work you have done consistently over a period of time—or some particular aspect of it. Narrate in the past tense. Begin with the time closest to the present and go back in time.

❺ Imagine yourself in your current life doing some task that allows you to think while working (washing dishes, weeding, painting a wall, etc.). While you do this task, you are thinking of an event from your childhood. Your description will move back and forth between the present scene and the past event. You will write four versions, each of which should be no more than two pages:

➤ Write it all in past tense.

➤ Write it all in present tense.

➤ Write "now" (you washing the dishes) in the present tense and "then" (the childhood event) in the past tense.

➤ Write "now" in the past tense and "then" in the present.

Don't try to make each version the same. Changes in tense should demand changes in how you tell the story.

❻ Write down the words "If only I had...," and see what story from your life they suggest. Now write that story, including how it would have been different "if only" you had....

7

Using
Your
Senses

f you have taken creative writing classes or read other books about creative writing, you have probably come across the "show, don't tell" maxim. And, in general, it is good advice: your writing will be far more engaging if you *show* your readers the particular squint in your father's left eye that appeared as he got angry, or if you *show* them the thumping of your mother's fist on an oak table before she burst into tears, than if you merely *tell* them that your father was prone to fits of anger or that your mother often cried out of frustration.

Sometimes beginning writers veer away from concrete details, worrying that by being too specific their story won't be "universal." But it is precisely in the particular details of one person's story that the writing opens itself up to its readers, allowing them to enter that story rather than stay at a distance, as they do when the writing is more abstract.

The key to writing that shows rather than tells is the senses. The very word "show" demands that the writing give the reader something to see: the sense of sight is invoked. But the other senses are important too, and, because they are more often overlooked than the sense of sight, they sometimes produce the most resonant images of all—images of smell or of sound that will stay with the reader long after he has finished the book. The Brooklyn apartment in Vivian Gornick's *Fierce Attachments*, for example, remains in my mind, not only as a place filled with the specific words of the women pulling in their clothes from lines strung across the alley but also as a place that quite surprisingly both smelled and tasted of green:

> *Yet I remember the alley as a place of clear light and sweet air, suffused, somehow, with a perpetual smell of summery green.*

And a page later:

> *I leaned out the kitchen window with a sense of expectancy I can still taste in my mouth, and that taste is colored a tender and brilliant green.*

Like places, characters come alive when you pick the particularly telling detail that can make the difference between a cardboard character and a real, live person. This is not a matter of throwing an abundance of details—say, of a person's visual appearance—at the reader, but of selecting those few that capture the essence of that person. The perfect one may be a quirk of speech, a mannerism, the way his hair falls across his face, an item of clothing, the smell of her, or how she walks.

Descriptive details are not simply a matter of using adjectives and adverbs—indeed, you will arrive at stronger descriptive writing if you banish almost all of them. All too often these modifiers repeat what has been conveyed by the noun or verb ("red strawberries" or "blared loudly"). Sometimes adjectives sit in front of nouns in pairs, when one more carefully chosen would suffice. Often the descriptive information given in an adjective can be better covered by a lively verb (compare, for example, the sentence "It was a hot, sultry afternoon" with

"The afternoon blazed and sweated") or a more precise noun (compare "He could barely see in the dim light after sunset" with "He could barely see in the dusk"). The same is true for adverbs, which can often be eliminated in favor of a better verb (compare "he walked quickly" with "he strode," "he paced," etc.).

When you intersperse good descriptive details throughout your writing, the reader becomes familiar with certain characters through his own encounters with them. As he reads, he gets to know and understand them himself, rather than being told everything that's important about them in an initial summary description. It works best when it is like real life, in which we get to know people gradually, as we piece together the

CONCRETE AND ABSTRACT

Concrete nouns are those that can be experienced by one (or more) of the five senses: sight, hearing, smell, taste, and touch.

Poppies, whisper, bacon, chocolate, and *skin,* are all concrete nouns. Concrete nouns are likely to make your writing lively and rich.

Abstract nouns are those that can be experienced only in the mind. They are ideas.

Beauty, evil, anger, confusion, and *love,* are all abstract nouns. Abstract nouns are likely to make your writing dull.

Concrete nouns tend to go with showing; abstract nouns tend to go with telling.

If you find yourself using an abstract noun, such as beauty, ask yourself how you can show the reader that beauty, rather than telling him it exists. Think in terms of concrete examples. If you show the beauty, you won't have to use the word.

things we find out about them. Although in memoir you are the narrator musing on the people, places, and events in your life, for it to work as a story your readers must, to some degree, make their own acquaintance with the characters through the sensory details you provide.

One of the many gifts of Maya Angelou's famous memoir, *I Know Why the Caged Bird Sings*, is her vivid description, full of sensory details, of the inhabitants of Stamps, Arkansas, where the author grew up, as in the following examples:

> *Mr. McElroy, who lived in the big rambling house next to the store, was very tall and broad, and although the years had eaten away the flesh from his shoulders, they had not, at the time of my knowing him, gotten to his high stomach, or his hands or feet.*

And:

> *On my way into church, I saw Sister Monroe, her open-faced gold crown glinting when she opened her mouth to return a neighborly greeting.*

And:

> *Mrs. Bertha Flowers was the aristocrat of Black Stamps. She had the grace of control to appear warm in the coldest weather, and on the Arkansas summer days it seemed she had a private breeze which swirled around, cooling her. She was thin without the taut look of wiry people, and her printed voile dresses and flowered hats were as right for her as denim overalls for a farmer.*

Places, too, can be revealed in this way to the reader if you select the sensory details that best characterize them, rather than the generalities that so often creep into descriptions of landscape. Dorothy Allison's language is as specific and unsentimental in this description of her birthplace in *Two or Three*

Things I Know for Sure as it is in the writing about her family (and notice the energy in the verbs):

> *Where I was born—Greenville, South Carolina—smelled like nowhere else I've ever been. Cut wet grass, split green apples, baby shit and beer bottles, cheap makeup and motor oil. Everything was ripe, everything was rotting. Hound dogs butted my calves. People shouted in the distance; crickets boomed in my ears. That country was beautiful, I swear to you, the most beautiful place I've ever been. Beautiful and terrible. It is the country of my dreams and the country of my nightmares: a pure pink and blue sky, red dirt, white clay, and all that endless green— willows and dogwood and firs going on for miles.*

❧ ❧ ❧

Lucy Grealy's memoir, *Autobiography of a Face*, takes as its theme the author's struggle with disfigurement as a result of cancer, and the many surgeries and medical procedures she underwent during childhood and adolescence to rebuild her face. It might have been tempting to "spare" the reader some of the painful sensory details, yet it is these very details that make the writing powerful. Abstractions or distance in a story like Grealy's would have reduced it to an account of something the reader would be likely to shy away from. But Grealy does not deal in abstractions, going literally deep inside herself for details, as in this description of chemotherapy:

> *It was an anatomy lesson. I had never known it was possible to feel your organs, feel them the way you feel your tongue in your mouth, or your teeth. My stomach outlined itself for me; my intestines, my liver, parts of me I didn't know the names of began heating up, trembling with their own warmth, creating friction and space by rubbing against the viscera, the muscles of my stomach, my back, my lungs. I wanted to collapse, to fall back*

onto the table or, better yet, go head first down onto the cold floor, but I couldn't. The injection had only begun; this syringe was still half full and there was a second one to go.

It might also have been tempting for the author to spare herself the pain of reliving such memories. Whether the memories involve physical or emotional pain, each memoirist must be prepared to be touched by events she may think have long since lost the power to affect her. Some, like Louis Gates, Jr., after writing *Colored People*, find that the writing actually brings up long-buried memories, which then have to be dealt with, sometimes, as in Gates's case, in therapy. It is frequently the writing of specific, sensory detail, rather than any conscious analysis on the part of the writer, that opens up for both writer and reader the meaning—and sometimes the pain— underneath the descriptive surface.

For me, sensory detail became crucial to finding the deeper layers of my memoir *Lifesaving*, which on one level was about three years I spent living in Spain in my early twenties, but which, on all the deeper levels, was about grief, coming of age, loneliness, and sexual identity. I started writing that book by telling the often-funny stories of being the only foreigner living in a small market town in Catalonia in the midsixties. There were portraits of local characters, lively stories of fiestas, and accounts of my work life as tour guide to a castle and winery. Yet, the story I really wanted to write was very different. It involved the fact that my parents had both been killed in a maritime disaster six months earlier; that I had barely shed a tear and was unable to begin grieving because I was alone; and that I had gone to Spain partly to escape the frightening fact of falling in love with another woman in the midst of all this disaster.

When, finally, those deeper themes began to unfold in my book, it was always the sensory details that opened the way. In a chapter about water—the sudden rains that led to flooding at the coast—I moved closer and closer to the water itself, until I described myself sitting outdoors, drenched by the pouring rain. Quite unexpectedly, the physicality of this description moved the writing toward the unshed tears that threatened to engulf me, just as the sudden storms engulfed carelessly parked cars and swept them out to sea. In a chapter about an older woman who worked at the winery, I discovered, through my description of her legs and her body size, that she had entered my life—and now my story—because of her physical likeness to my dead mother. And in trying to describe the exact sounds of raucous Catalan speech heard in the market and on the beach, I reawakened memories of family vacations on those same beaches before my parents' deaths.

Memory resides in specific sensory details, not in abstract notions like "beautiful" or "angry" (ask yourself, "in what particular way was she beautiful?" or "what did the angry dog sound like?") If we can capture and name the particular smell of the wax polish in that long-ago house, then other memories seem to follow.

When Jill Ker Conway wants to remember an event, she starts with where the chairs were in the room. Toni Morrison calls this "emotional memory—what the nerves and the skin remember as well as how it appeared." Russell Baker says he remembers very well the day of his father's death. Although he was only five at the time, Baker was able to tap into vivid memories for his memoir *Growing Up* because of the sensory details that have stayed with him: "I can still hear people talking that day. I know what the air smelled like. I know what people's faces looked like. How they were dressed. What they were eating."

Not only can a sensory detail be a key to memories, it can also offer a way into the writing—a clue to its eventual shape. Points of entry are vital to find, though their nature varies from writer to writer. For some, the way in may be the rhythm of a phrase or sentence; for others it's a snatch of dialogue; and for many, it's a smell, a sound, or a sight. For Ian Frazier, setting out to write *Family*, it was objects: the right artifacts, he says, suggested narrative. For me, it is sometimes a sensory image, as it was when I wrote a short memoir called "Fish." The piece ended up being about the hidden conflicts between the men and the women in my family, as well as my own confusion about which side to identify with, but the written memoir starts with me at a kitchen sink in Spain holding a small knife, with a row of fish laid out waiting to be gutted. The smell of those fish fresh from the fishing boat and the way they looked with their opaque, staring eyes were the way in to both the memories and the memoir.

If you find yourself having trouble getting into a story you want to tell, it is always a good idea to get up very close and start using your senses. You may have a good idea of the whole story in your mind, but your vision of the whole may, in fact, be a hindrance to finding the way in. Describing some of the details, using your ears and eyes, calling up a smell that belongs to the story, or reaching an imaginary hand back through time to touch a piece of furniture, or the texture of a dress, or someone's skin—these acts of memory will serve you well. They can and should be exercised over and over, not only to get you going, but also to push your story deeper, pull your reader closer, and lift the heart of the story out of obscurity into a sensory world that you and your readers can inhabit together.

❶ Choose a house you have lived in and know well. Write a sensory description of that house, paying attention to all five senses.

❷ Pick another place—interior or exterior—and describe it in detail, focusing on *one* sense that is not sight.

❸ Write a two-page portrait of someone you knew or know well, using all possible senses. What did he or she sound like? (Not just speech, but other sounds.) What smells followed him or her? Are there textures you can remember from body or clothes?

❹ Write another two-page portrait, this time seeing if you can select sensory details that show how you feel or felt about the person. Try not to tell.

❺ Pick a day or part of a day from your memory and assign it a color. Describe that time, returning to, and developing, the theme of color and showing the reader why you think of it as a "yellow day" or a "purple afternoon."

Naming
Names

The names of people, places, stores, rivers, and so on are a particular kind of concrete detail that can play a vital role in making your writing interesting and believable. In some cases, the name itself carries layers of history and imagery more apt than any image the writer could add.

Ursula K. Le Guin's "Places Names," (I wouldn't know whether to describe it as poem, essay, or memoir) contains many lists of the names of places encountered while driving across the country. Even if he has never been anywhere near these places, the reader sees a great deal more than an anonymous list of names, since the names themselves resonate with the history of the place, as in this section, where the narrator has just reached the Allegheny River:

> *Snow Bird Road*
> *Smithburg*
> *Englands Run*
> *Morgans Run*
> *Buckeye Run*
> *Dark Hollow*

Fort New Salem
Dog Run
Cherry Camp
Raccoon Run
Salem Fork
Flinderation.

The names of places often reveal a history of invasion and colonization. In James Hamilton-Paterson's *The Great Deep: The Sea and Its Thresholds*, there is a chapter entitled, "Nothing Is More Tedious than a Landscape without Names." The author refers specifically to the fact that many geographical features of the ocean bed are named: there is, for example, a whole region north of Hawaii containing the Musicians Seamounts, which include Mt. Strauss, Mt. Mendelssohn, Bach and Beethoven Ridges, and a mountain slightly taller than Mount Fuji named Mozart. The reader can see from these names that the naming of the sea bed is being done, not by the people who live in the vicinity of the named features, but by the Western oceanographers who "discover" them.

Sometimes certain place names acquire a resonance in the context of a particular narrator's story, as in Jamaica Kincaid's memoir, "On Seeing England for the First Time." Kincaid, who grew up black in Antigua, describes her first visit to England in a narrative interwoven with memories of being made to feel inferior as a black child in a British colony. The white cliffs of Dover are a famous landmark that appears in nostalgic English songs and stories, but when this landmark is named at the end of Kincaid's memoir, it becomes a symbol of all that is valued simply because it is white:

> *The moment I wished every sentence, everything I knew, that began with England would end with "and then it all died, we don't know how, it just all died" was when I saw the white cliffs of Dover. I had sung hymns and recited poems that were about a*

longing to see the white cliffs of Dover again. At the time I sang
the hymns and recited the poems, I could really long to see them
again because I had never seen them at all, nor had anyone
around me at the time. But there we were, groups of people long-
ing for something we had never seen. And so there they were, the
white cliffs, but they were not that pearly majestic thing I used
to sing about, that thing that created such a feeling in these
people that when they died in the place where I lived they had
themselves buried facing a direction that would allow them to see
the white cliffs of Dover when they were resurrected, as surely
they would be. The white cliffs of Dover, when finally I saw them,
were cliffs, but they were not white; you would only call them
that if the word "white" meant something special to you; they
were dirty and they were steep; they were so steep, the correct
height from which all my views of England, starting with the
map before me in my classroom and ending with the trip I had
just taken, should jump and die and disappear forever.

Place names also carry linguistic music. The Indian names
close to where I live, such as Multnomah, Clackamas,
Snohomish, Clatskanie, and Wallowa resonate very differently
than those with settlers' names like Portland or Salem. Ethnic
origins are revealed through names like The Dalles, Willamette
and Grande Ronde, or El Paso and Rio Grande, while ubiqui-
tous names like Main Street in the U.S. or High Street in Britain are reminders of a commonality held by towns in a national
culture.

Names of cities, streets, buildings, rivers, and so on, not
only carry history and image within them, they also convince
a reader that the writer knows what she is talking about. As
you set out to tell a story, it is vital for the reader to put himself
in your hands. Naming names is one way you can win that
reader's trust and give your voice authority. This is from
Patricia Hampl's *Virgin Time:*

*Lexington, Oxford, Chatsworth, continuing down Grand
Avenue to Milton and Avon, as far as St. Albans—the streets of
our neighborhood had an English, even an Anglican, ring to
them. But we were Catholic. The parishes of the diocese, un-
marked and ghostly as they were, posted borders more decisive
than the street signs we passed on our way to St. Luke's grade
school or, later, walking in the other direction to the girls' only
convent high school.*

*We were like people with dual citizenship. I lived on Linwood
Avenue, but I belonged to St. Luke's. That was the lingo. Mothers spoke of daughters who were going to the junior-senior prom
with boys "from Nativity" or "from St. Mark's" as if from
fiefdoms across the sea.*

*"Where you from?" a boy livid with acne asked when we
startled each other lurking behind a pillar in the St. Thomas
Academy gym at Friday-night freshman mixer.*

*"Ladies' choice!" one of the mothers cried from a dim corner
where a portable hi-fi was set up. She rasped the needle over the
vinyl, and Fats Domino came on, insinuating a heavier pleasure
than I yet knew:* I found my thrill...

*"I'm from Holy Spirit," the boy said, as if he'd been beamed
in to stand by the tepid Cokes and tuna sandwiches and the
bowls of sweating potato chips on the refreshments table.*

This opening can hardly fail to convince the reader that the
author knows a great deal about her subject: she knows street
names and parish names; she knows which direction to walk
to grade school and high school; she knows the lingo that
people used to discuss these things; she knows the exact night
of the freshman mixer and what was on the refreshments table;
and she knows the song, and some of its actual words, that
played on the hi-fi. She manages, too, to give this copious information in story form. The reader does not feel he is being
given a ton of background information, but rather that a story
is beginning to unfold. He enters into that story in part because

of concrete images such as "livid with acne," and "lurking behind a pillar." Thus, the writer wins both the trust and interest
of the reader in a few short paragraphs.

Here is another opening paragraph, this one from Evelyn C.
White's memoir, "Ode to Aretha":

> *The last time I talked to Aretha Franklin we exchanged a few*
> *words about Coretta Scott King. It was in the fall of 1981, after*
> *Aretha had given a spine-tingling concert at Radio City Music*
> *Hall in New York City. By telling the security staff that I was*
> *Martin Luther King's daughter, I had gained entry to the back-*
> *stage room where the Queen of Soul stood in a muted black tux-*
> *edo and fluffy pink house shoes.*

Here, the author needs to establish her authority even while
asking the reader to believe that she once bluffed her way into
Aretha's backstage party by pretending to be Martin Luther
King's daughter. Part of how she establishes the necessary authoritative voice is by using immediately recognizable names:
Aretha Franklin, Coretta Scott King, Radio City Music Hall in
New York City, Martin Luther King and the Queen of Soul, all
in the space of a few lines. In addition, she is satisfyingly specific about the year and about what she and Aretha talked
about. Notice, too, that she finds room for a sensory image,
showing the reader Aretha in her black tuxedo and pink house
shoes. Who could doubt she knows what she's talking about?

❍ ❍ ❍

A name—real or otherwise—is what lifts the writing out of
generalization and anonymity. Patricia Hampl introduces the
next-door neighbors of her childhood thus:

> *As for the Bertrams, our nearest neighbors to the west, it could*
> *only be said that Mrs. Bertram, dressed in a narrow suit with a*

peplum jacket and a hat made of the same heathery wool, went
somewhere via taxi on Sunday mornings. Mr. Bertram went
nowhere—on Sunday or on any other day. He was understood,
during my entire girlhood, to be indoors, resting.

It turns out there's a lot more to be said about the Bertrams, but even if this had been all Hampl told us about them, they would be far more vivid characters because they are named than they would be unnamed. Nothing would pull the reader into: "As for our nearest neighbors to the west, it could only be said that *she* (or *the wife*) dressed in a narrow suit.... *He* (or *the husband*) went nowhere...." Without names, they remain generic rather than specific. As "the Bertrams," on the other hand, they are real live neighbors, living, breathing characters in the story. It really doesn't matter to the reader if "Bertram" was their real name or not. But it might matter a lot to the Bertrams.

The next chapter deals with the difficulties of writing about living people, and legal issues are dealt with in the appendix to this book. For now, though, as you work on your memoirs, go right ahead and name names.

❶ Think of a place where you lived as a child. Generate a list of names associated with that place, such as street names, districts, geographical features: rivers, meadows, farms, mountains, woods, etc. Include the names of stores, businesses, public buildings, and anything else you can think of that has a name. After you have finished listing, start to write memories of living in that place, allowing the names to enter the narrative.

❷ Pick an age between eight and fifteen. Focus on being that age and list the names of ten people who were part of your life, excluding parents, grandparents, and siblings. Think of friends, peers, teachers, grownups you knew from different contexts. Write down their names as you thought of them *at that time:* "Mrs. Atkins" (teacher), "Jody's mom," "Uncle Bill," etc. Now read this list aloud to someone else and ask him or her to pick one. (If no one is available, close your eyes and point a pencil at the list.) Generate as much detail as you can about that person in the form of notes, then select from your notes to create a portrait not more than two pages long.

❸ Write short portraits of the other people from the list you made in #2.

❹ Think of a street name from a place you once lived. Describe that street in great detail. List stores or houses, anyone you know who lived there, things you remember happening on that street.

❺ Think of someone you once knew well but haven't seen for several years. Write about him or her, starting with "the last time I talked to...."

❻ Think of the name of a place or landmark that you like because of the *sound* of the name. (Mississippi, Snohomish, Cadaqués, Firle Beacon, and Windmill Hill are some of mine.) Write about that landmark, focusing on the sound and its associations.

9

Writing about Living People

*S*ome writers, wrestling with the inner and outer voices that urge them to stay silent, become defiant: we have a *right* to our truths, they say to themselves or to anyone who wants to debate the question with them. And indeed they do. However, writers who have plenty to say about their rights to free speech are sometimes less anxious to think about the responsibilities that go along with those rights. This chapter deals with the ethical questions that surround writing about living people; legal aspects are discussed in the appendix.

We must each come to our own decisions about the writer's responsibility to those whose lives are entwined with our own, and whose stories inevitably overlap with ours. You might be writing about a failed relationship. Perhaps your memoir involves your closeted gay brother, your teenage daughter's first period, or a close friend's mental breakdown. Each of us must balance the reasons for writing a story or for using real names, against the harm that might be done to someone else. Sometimes the choice is not difficult to make: you believe that your story will be crucial to many readers, and that any harm to others will be slight. But often it is harder to know what matters most: someone's livelihood or your need to tell the story; the importance of your story to many readers or one person's fear of public humiliation.

Rather than getting stuck in an either/or situation, I always try to remember that there may be a solution that satisfies both values—there are often options beyond the simple choice of telling or not telling. I can, for example, be selective about what to include, allowing my selections to be influenced by a genuine desire not to harm someone in my story. I can, if I choose, show my writing to the person in question and find out exactly how he or she feels about its publication. I can change names or identifying characteristics. I can also decide not to worry about any of this until I've written the story and am thinking about publishing.

If you do face these difficult choices, a good question to ask yourself is: Which decision is most life enhancing? Colluding with a system of denial that allows for the continuation of abuse or exploitation, whether it be in a family or a workplace, is not life enhancing. It is quite the opposite—though individuals who are part of that system may try to convince you that *their* lives are at stake. But revealing something that can damage someone else's life because that person is vulnerable to unjust retribution or is emotionally fragile, may, in some circumstances be simply irresponsible on your part. In these kinds of situations, I feel certain that, if faced with an unresolvable conflict, peoples' lives are more important than my words.

While we sometimes tend to overestimate the power of our words to get other people—or ourselves—into trouble, there are situations that do warrant our informed concern. I have a friend, for example, who is writing about her time as a teacher in China. Writing about friends she made there is fraught with difficulties that may not be solved even by changing names, descriptions, and locations. In China, associating with someone from the West is frowned upon, and having that association made public in a book could result in her friends losing jobs, being denied access to decent housing, or losing their right to leave the country. Her words could even conceivably land someone in jail.

Publishing true stories about Mexican illegal immigrants, gay teachers, or a doctor who assisted in a suicide, we can become responsible for someone's deportation or job loss, financial ruin or social ostracism, if our characters are recognizable. Many Americans are ignorant of immigration laws, unaware of the pervasive nature of homophobia, and unwilling to acknowledge the prejudice that can strike down the very people we admire. But, as writers, it is our business to understand fully what can happen to people when we reveal what we know about them.

Writing about those who have hurt us is a different matter. We may find ourselves not caring, or even delighting in, the consequences to family members, priests, medical professionals, teachers, and others who have abused their power over us in the past. But we should beware of revenge as a motive. Writing that has retaliation as its goal is always transparent, and makes readers uncomfortable. Although anger may be what gets you started, the writing will not flourish until you give your full allegiance to the story itself, letting go of your wish to use your writing to gain sympathy from readers or to hurt someone. In this situation, weighing your responsibility toward the people in your story is particularly difficult, and you should wait until you are thinking about publication, by which time you may be better able to come to a decision.

Memoirists vary enormously in their responses to the dilemmas that arise around family. Jill Ker Conway, for example, couldn't have written *The Road from Coorain* while her mother was alive. "She would have struck me dead," she says. And in *An American Childhood* Annie Dillard simply tried to leave out anything that might trouble her family. "Everybody I'm writing about," she says, "is alive and well, in full possession of his faculties, and possibly willing to sue. Things were simpler when I wrote about muskrats." Russell Baker simply said to his wife, "Read through it, and if there's anything you want cut, I'll cut it."

For Teresa Jordan, it was initially less clear how to relate to family members when she wrote her memoir *Riding the White Horse Home*, a story of her Western ranching family. "It was extremely hard to start writing about my family," she said, when I talked with her about it.

> *The ranching world is a very private world: you don't complain and you don't tell anybody your secrets.*
>
> *The book came very slowly. It was like pulling teeth. At first I did not intend to write about living people. It was going to be a series of essays, the first one being about rugged individualism. It was a scholarly project involving letters of pioneers. But one thing led to another and I wrote an anecdote about my grandfather. When I sent it to my editor, he said "this is what you're supposed to be writing about."*
>
> *I sent the work to my father and brother, feeling that if they had problems with it I wouldn't publish. In fact, it opened up a conversation with my father. He seemed to feel relief, as if he felt understood. Although at that time I was willing not to publish if he felt it was too private, I'm not sure I feel that way any more.*
>
> *What I have to decide is, what is my story to tell? My story includes other people of course. I think that if you understand the true depth of the story, it's surprising how much truth people will embrace about themselves. If a story seems too personal, it's often because it's not resolved enough for the writer—the writer is asking the reader for too much: for things like understanding or pity. Or perhaps the writer is writing to settle a score with someone in the story. You can certainly write about people who have hurt you if you're not trying to manipulate them.*
>
> *Writers are users. We do use the stories around us. I feel that carries a huge responsibility. I try to work with people openly,*

and in my own memoir it was important to me to show it to my family, but I can certainly imagine situations in which you would decide not to do that.

Whether or not we feel obliged to involve our families in the process, these questions are often painful ones. Sallie Bingham's memoir, *Passion and Prejudice*, tells with great candor the story of her rich and powerful family, her male relatives' sexism, and the hurtful way in which she was ousted from the family's newspaper empire. No one reading this could suppose it was easy to resist the pressure exerted by such a family to keep quiet. Bingham writes of her mother's response to her digging up an old family secret from the past:

> *By now I was struggling to control my tears, and she was about to get out of the car. I asked her why the scandal surrounding Mary Lily's death, more than seventy years earlier, was more important to her than her relationship with me.*
>
> *She replied that it was a question of honor, and got out of the car. She added that they would not see me until after my book was published.*
>
> *I felt nearly obliterated by pain. It brought in its wake feelings of helplessness and terror that must have been familiar to an infant girl crying for food and love. For a while it seemed as though I could not survive the isolation Mother was imposing; nor could I expose myself to another attempt, which would inevitably, I believed, bring rejection and hours of weeping and despair.*

Extreme though this pain was, it should be noted that Bingham moved through it and came, relatively soon, to understand her family's fears and to go ahead with the book anyway:

> *They cannot write me out, as Mary Lily was written out, silence me, or reward me into compliance.*

It is the loss of power that is most frightening for people like my parents. It means that reality is cresting, about to burst their limits.

What is love, compared to that fearful flood?

Of course, writing about living people is not always a problem. Sometimes it has positive consequences, as it did in Teresa Jordan's case with her father. Jill Ker Conway, who believes it to be an invasion of privacy not to show the relevant sections of her books to the people mentioned, sent her brother parts of *The Road from Coorain*. She told him she would not publish the book if he found it too painful, but he responded favorably and encouraged her to keep going with it. Ian Frazier also asked permission of almost everybody in his memoir, *Family*, and came to the conclusion that most people really do want to be written about. Like Jordan, he felt that they wanted to be known and remembered.

Most of my memoirs have dealt with family, and some might say I've had it easy since both my parents are dead. Certainly I haven't had to worry about their reactions, although I have sometimes worried about the way I have used their deaths in my work. But I have other living relatives, mostly of the kind that prefer not to discuss feelings. This makes it all too apparent that I shouldn't discuss my own feelings in print, but I do it anyway. Their reticence makes life after publication more peaceful than it might be in some other families, but their silent approval or disapproval is, of course, a factor I carry around in my head. I have to drum up a certain defiance while I am writing, and particularly when I publicly read aloud pieces from my memoirs; I have to remind myself that I am not doing something embarrassing or disloyal. Time and again, I battle my family's prohibition on intimacy, telling myself that it is important that we know one another and be known.

More recently I have been working on memoirs about my involvement with feminist politics in London in the seventies—a hotbed of opinionated, passionate women, none of whom will be at all reticent when I go public with my version of those days. I show pieces to friends and listen to how they think I got it wrong. Sometimes I am influenced, but, in the long run, among all the many stories that could be told about that time, I know I have my own to tell.

Whatever we decide, the most important thing is that each of us think carefully about these questions. We have a right to tell our stories, but not to blunder into publication without a thought for the consequences. "No rights without responsibilities" is not a popular principle, yet we must accept it if our writing is to be a power for good.

❶ Write a portrait of someone you hate, knowing that person will never see it.

❷ Write about how it would feel if the person described in #1 *did* see your portrait of him/her.

❸ Tell the story of something in your life you are ashamed of.

❹ Write about how you would feel about people you know reading a story from #3. Then write about how you would feel if a complete stranger read it. When you have finished, know that you don't have to show any of this to anybody.

❺ List any events or people you would not write about if your writing were to be published. For each one, write at least a page about why you feel this way.

❻ Write about one of the events or people listed in #5, knowing no one need read what you write. When you have finished, note whether you have anything to add to your thoughts on why this could not be published. Note, too, whether there are ways you could change the story in order to disguise people and make it publishable.

10

Your Memoir
and the
World

f you're not careful, you can shut out the world too completely. Memoir needs to be a very personal story and is bound to lead you inward. Working on your story can sometimes pull you into greater and greater communion with your psyche, until your narrative becomes stranded on the island of your personal life—stranded there with no connection at all to the mainland.

Although inner work is essential to the writing, at some point you must take a step back and read through what you have written, asking yourself if the story is grounded in the world beyond your personal life. This grounding is important for several reasons: first of all because it allows your reader to know where he is in time and in geography. Cultural references, such as current movies or pop songs, historical events, great sports moments, fashions in clothes or architecture, food fads, or modes of transportation, all provide clues about the setting of your story and place it in the public world. These details need not pull you outside the story; rather, you can weave them in, maintaining your vision and voice as you glance out of the window from the private story into the world beyond.

There is, of course, a danger of focusing *too much* on external events; it's easy to use them to avoid trudging down the inner road you suspect may lead to painful truths. You will want to find the right balance, to anchor your story in a wider world so that your readers can interact both with what is true specifically and uniquely for you, as well as with a world they recognize and share. Sometimes this is as simple as a reference to popular culture—Doctor Kildare on the TV, "Smoke Gets in Your Eyes" played over and over on the turntable—and sometimes it involves a lengthier foray into a well-known public or historical event that somehow intrudes upon, or is the bedrock for, your story.

Often the personal story will be given new layers of meaning if you make such a foray into the public arena. In Roxanne Dunbar Ortiz's memoir, *Red Dirt: Growing Up Okie,* for instance, the author describes herself at fourteen, in a time when the polio epidemic was sweeping across the country and locusts were eating the wheat fields around her home. Confined to the couch because of an asthma attack, she hears a radio report about the Rosenbergs, who are about to be executed for treason. The private and public worlds merge as the child tries to use each one to help understand the other: the locusts, according to the Baptist preacher, are a Biblical plague just like the polio that has smitten her cousin; the electricity that will kill the Rosenbergs is the same that enters her own house:

> *I tried to figure out how light bulbs might kill. Our house was hooked up to electricity, one wire that entered through a hole in the wall and was attached to one light bulb and to the radio. There was nothing else that required electricity. Electricity fascinated and scared me, like lightning or magic. So, I thought, maybe electricity could kill somebody. I imagined the Rosenbergs lit up like light bulbs, glowing, slowly burning from the heat. I thought it would take a long time to die that way. Our light bulbs died only after two months.*

The presence of a more public world, even if only in the form of a classroom, a hospital, a fairground, or a workplace,

INNER DIALOGUE

We usually think of dialogue as being a conversation between two (or more) people.

Inner dialogue, however, is a conversation you have with yourself. It's when you tell how you perceive something or feel about it—when you speculate to yourself about what happened, or play out in your mind how you wish it had gone. The reader experiences it as overhearing your thoughts. Or perhaps as a dialogue with *them* personally. (For an example, see excerpt from "Poetry and Prejudice" on page 147.)

Inner dialogue, like a dream, is sometimes hard to make accessible to the reader for the following reasons:

• Things that make perfect sense to you because you have been unraveling them and coming to understand them for years may not fall into place so easily for your reader.

• The language each of us uses, with its various metaphors for how we experience our inner worlds, varies enormously from person to person. Therefore, when I try to explain to you what a dream meant or precisely how I felt when I was confronted with my estranged lover, I may use imagery that to me perfectly portrays my inner responses but that to you is mystifying.

Inner dialogue can benefit enormously from feedback. Showing passages to selected readers and asking for honest, specific reactions, including their summary of what the passage says, can help you assess how well you have communicated your thoughts—how well your inner dialogue works when it is overheard.

often provides a point of entry for the reader into your story. Put yourself in your reader's shoes: is there a way in for him— something he recognizes as familiar, from which he can venture into the unfamiliar? If you rely on readers being able to identify only with the particulars of your private life, you are making it hard for them.

My memoir, "Poetry and Prejudice" presents a problem of identification for some readers, since it is set in the remote Wallowa Mountains of Oregon, in a rural Western culture that is certainly recognizable to some but may be fairly foreign to many, and since it deals with homophobia from the point of view of a lesbian. The personal story is one that requires many readers to make a giant stretch of identification, perhaps across barriers of hatred, discomfort, or ignorance. Luckily, the story is set in a school, in a classroom that is probably recognizable to almost everyone in the U.S. When I have read this story aloud, teachers often come up to me and tell me their own classroom stories; others say they remember being a student in a class rather like this one.

> The ten boys overflowed from chairs and desks, long legs in skintight blue jeans sprawled forward with the pointed toes of their cowboy boots sticking up defiantly, as if giving me the finger. The two girls giggled together and never finished writing anything, but screwed up their papers and threw them away in loud disgust, as if to reassure the boys over and over that they had appropriately low expectations of themselves. At first, seeing how outnumbered they were, I had felt sorry for them, but by now I was exasperated....

> For the next ten minutes there was a lot of squirming, writing, balling up of paper, and giggling. I tried to write too, as I always do, using my own assignments to generate lines or images that I might use later. But I found it hard to concentrate in the atmosphere, which was anything but peaceful. The two girls, who were sitting in front, whispered to each other until I stared

at them, when they pouted and looked at their paper, but made it clear they were just waiting till I looked away so they could resume their conversation.

For many readers, this point of common experience is the way into the story. Having invited them in by this route, I then move into some very internal, purely personal subject matter about my response to the homophobic incident, the impact of which only works on them if they are already willing to be there in that room.

> *The first thought that came into my head was that if I told them I was a lesbian I would not be physically safe in the cabin. There was no phone there and I was one of only a handful of inhabitants up at the lake this early in the season. I could already see the pickup truck full of rowdy boys with a couple of guns in the rack, hurtling down the track in the dark; I imagined the headlights penetrating the living room windows as it swung onto the grass in front of the cabin; I knew how their big, competent hands would hold the knives and guns they had been writing about all week. Then it flashed through my mind that there would be other repercussions: in this contract work, which I relied on for a significant part of my income, it would be easy to phase me out—I wouldn't have to be fired; I just wouldn't get invited back to any of the schools up here when word got around.*
>
> *It certainly wasn't my first confrontation with homophobia, yet it entered my body in a way that was different from anything I had encountered before. As the laughter tore around me, it was as if the outrage I had politely suppressed throughout my life was suddenly unlocked...and the kind of frustration that makes you want to be a baby, yelling and waving your fists, all pulsed through my bloodstream. I felt hot enough to explode.*

This internal dialogue continues for another page, after which I describe more of the external scene in the classroom, thus reminding the reader of the familiar context for this very personal, and to some, unfamiliar, experience.

Carolyn See's memoir, *Dreaming: Hard Luck and Good Times in America*, focuses heavily on personal life with much internal exploration. Her book is a study of how alcohol and drugs affected her family, and consequently her whole life. Although much takes place within the walls of the writer's intensely private experience, there are also forays into public worlds such as school. Later in the book, still focusing on personal relationships, the author describes her marriages and adult life, bringing in the larger picture when she describes the California hippie values of the sixties. Many readers of a certain age will recognize the scene:

> *Our living room was long and narrow—23 by about 10 feet, the house cut in half lengthwise. We ate at one end, under a bright pink bookcase with one shelf taken out so it could hold our tree of life. We must have eaten either fish soup or chicken-and-sausage stew. We listened to Ravi Shankar. Trees scratched at the windows and raccoons looked in. The place was lit by candles and it glowed. We were stoned out of our minds. When it came time for dessert, I brought out a board with cheese and fruit. Terri started to cry. "It's just so beautiful," she said. And it was.*

In addition to grounding the reader and providing a way in to your memoir, the presence of the public world will add to the authenticity of your story. In a way, it becomes more *true* as you add more layers. After all, you didn't live that personal experience in a vacuum: it *did* take place in a social, political, geographical, and cultural context. Although you may have felt marooned in your childhood, as an adult using a retrospective voice, you can place that childhood in the world of a neighborhood, a school, acquaintances and friends, radio or television, and all the unexpected changes in the larger world that enter into a home. Readers know that children can be oblivious to such things but are unlikely to warm to an adult narrator who writes with the child's limited vision.

In order to ground your story in the world that surrounded it, you will have to be willing to extend your examined life beyond the purely personal. Not only must you do the hard work of understanding your own experience but you must also try to see how that experience was affected by the time you lived in, the particular strand of society you belonged to, and the values that were important in your community. As a reliable and interesting adult narrator, you must also have some opinions about these things, whether or not you directly address them in your story.

Do not, however, mistake this expanded vision for a loosening of the boundaries you have set around your story. Looking *outward* at the world that impinged upon that story does not require you to look *sideways* at a bigger slice of your experience. It requires only that you add layers to the story you have already identified.

๑ ๑ ๑

Look at the range of possibilities, from purely personal to public information. In the diagram on the following page, the shaded circles are those that pertain only to the author (and some to her immediate family) and are therefore private. The unshaded circles move outward through areas that are personal yet will be shared by some readers, into the mostly public domain. In each of these circles the author shares some experience with some readers—in general sharing more as she moves out from the center.

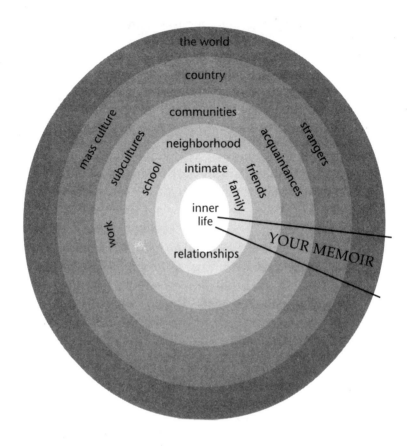

The memoir can enter any of these circles, and ideally will move back and forth between them or show how they are layered one on top of the other, as demonstrated by the slice through the circle marked "your memoir." Even when the subject matter is less personal (the outer circles), the personal voice is always what carries the reader from private life into the public world and back again. The personal voice is what the reader comes to trust. It is the sturdy vehicle that will carry him from the most intimate corners of the writer's childhood into the wide open spaces of a shared culture.

❶ Think of an event of historic or cultural importance that you remember (assassination of President Kennedy; the first moon landing; the end of the Berlin Wall; John Lennon's death; an outstanding sporting event, the March on Washington; the Roe v. Wade decision; the polio epidemic of the 1950s, the eruption of Mt. St. Helens, etc.). Write personally about how you witnessed or heard about that event and how it impacted you.

❷ Write four pages about life in your family in a particular year, making major references to the culture that entered your home (music, TV shows, food fads, radio, books, magazines, fashion, games, arts, etc.).

❸ Write no more than four pages about a major step in your understanding of yourself: an insight about your own psyche or a journey through confusion to clarity. This will be largely inner focused. Now add no more than another two pages (integrated into the previous work) that bring in the external world.

❹ Write four pages about your spiritual life: religious education or lack thereof, or independent spiritual exploration. Combine inner dialogue—your thoughts and feelings—with external settings and events.

❺ Write about a book (or movie or play, etc.) that was very important in your life. Combine information about the book for a reader who has never read it, with an exploration of how it impacted you personally.

❻ In three pages, describe a job you have had. Include coworkers, the work itself and its relationship to the world at large, how you felt about it, how it affected your life.

Watch Out
for the
Myths

Writing, like other creative and artistic pursuits, tends to be romanticized by many and vilified by some. Writers in the U.S. are seen as special, peculiar but mystical people whose lives have a certain magical charm, or, alternately, as drunken, neurotic wastrels who sponge off the government and do no work. Sometimes, unhappily, writers themselves perpetuate these myths. Many of the myths apply to all creative writers (technical writers are perceived to be more diligent, perhaps because they deal with facts rather than the imagination). A few apply specifically to memoirists.

You certainly don't have to be famous or infamous to write a memoir, yet the myth persists that if you are writing one you must be someone who has hit the headlines, or you must be related to such a person. Although the memoir is very popular at the moment—part of the explosion of creative nonfiction—still the general public hasn't caught on to the fact that the term simply applies to beautiful prose writing about actual experience.

It follows, then, that this same public, when it discovers that you are not obviously famous, must explain your memoir writing in some other way. Memoirists, they may conclude, must be too full of themselves, self-preoccupied, overly self-important, narcissistic. Do not believe it (unless, of course you really *are* too full of yourself, self-preoccupied, etc.).

The most insidious myths about creative writers erode our ability to stay fully in touch with ourselves—an essential ingredient for writing a memoir. Good writing requires that we push ourselves to become more, not less, conscious. Yet from time to time, we convince ourselves that there are short cuts through painful consciousness or simple aids to reaching it more quickly. Alcohol is one such highly mythologized, dead-end path that has taken its toll on writers.

We have inherited far too many romantic accounts of the anguished or suicidal writer alone in her room with a typewriter and several bottles of booze. Some will remember the movie in which Lillian Hellman (played by Jane Fonda) smokes, drinks, and throws her typewriter out of the window, or the poems in which Dorothy Parker focuses her acerbic wit on the plight of the tormented writer; others will have seen a current brochure for an artists' colony, with its glossy photo of the writer sitting amidst balled-up papers, the inevitable half-empty bottle of Scotch on the floor beside the desk. Continuing this tradition, we contemporary writers turn our own trials and errors, our own escape mechanisms and self-destructiveness, into dramatic stories, thus adding to the literature of romantic despair.

Many of us have been encouraged in these habits by irresponsible writing teachers who themselves have bought the myths and been shaped by them. I'll never forget many years ago, arriving at the first class offered by a moderately famous poet, to find her and her boyfriend cozily seated at a desk, thigh to thigh, with four gallons of wine and a tower of paper cups in front of them. Bravely, I stuck it out for the first half of the session, as student after student read aloud poems that sounded more and more like those of the famous poet, in speech that grew progressively more slurred. Then I read my poem, which sounded not at all like those of the famous poet. Three lines into it, the famous poet's boyfriend got up and walked out noisily. Five minutes later, I left and didn't return. With models like this, the neophyte writer may eagerly set herself up with a computer, lots of solitude, a doomed relationship, and a supply of cheap wine, which will very quickly produce the despair that she considers another essential ingredient in her chosen career.

Some writers mythologize our pervasive insecurities, falling under the spell of their own eloquence to make our fears seem both humorous and somehow appealing. In her book on writing, *Bird by Bird*, Anne Lamott is just one of many who write in this vein about the agony of sending off a manuscript:

> *Finally, if you are lucky, a week later you get a note from your agent's assistant that the manuscript has in fact arrived, and maybe one of the friends has called to say that he or she has read part of it and that it is just terrific and not to worry, but you go ahead and have a small breakdown anyhow, waiting for your agent and editor to call and tell you that it's brilliant. Every time the phone rings, you sing, "Let it please be him, oh, dear God, it must be him." But it's not him, and then you die and go on a massive eating binge and think about what phonies most of your friends are.*

Although such writing offers valuable reassurance that we are not alone in our insecurity, it also attaches a certain glamour to the writer's anxieties. Agonies of approval-seeking are, in fact, not at all glamorous—they are massive distractions from the work itself and from the consciousness the writer needs in order to go on working.

Competitiveness and envy, like anxiety about rejection, undoubtedly exist to some degree among writers, but I am disturbed by pieces of writing like Bonnie Friedman's "Envy, the

REJECTION LETTERS

Rejection letters from magazines are not usually actual letters. More often they are "rejection slips"—small slips of paper with a (usually) polite printed message that says something like: "Thank you for sending us your work, but I'm afraid we can't use it in *The Threepenny Review* at present. Wendy Lesser, editor."

Sometimes editors will hand write something on this printed slip or letter, which can be heartening. Most often the handwritten note says something like: "Try us again!" This doesn't mean you will have any better chance next time, although if you persist, they may begin to recognize your name, which some people think gives your submission a better reading.

Here's a random sample of rejections I have received recently for work I submitted directly to magazines and journals. Rejections of work submitted by my agent tend to be detailed letters.

•My favorite rejection this year was from *Harper's*, where assistant editor Jim Nelson handwrote a delightful, appreciative, and complimentary letter that ended with: "…I wanted to thank you for sending it our way and let you know we're always looking for material for the "Readings" section, so you should feel free to try us again."

•Printed slip from *Poets On*: "Dear (my name written in), We found your poems to be: ☑Too long ❑Too short ❑Too late ❑Unrelated to the theme ❑Not our style ❑Very good and almost made it ❑Made it." This one also had a handwritten note from the editor saying, "It's a fine poem but unfortunately too long for us to handle at this point—sorry."

•A typed personal letter from the managing editors of a small literary magazine apologizing for misplacing a submission of mine made thirteen months earlier and just found. They enclosed guidelines and asked me to submit again!

Writer's Disease" (in the otherwise marvelous *Writing Past Dark*). In this essay, Friedman describes her own and other writers' pangs of jealousy when some other writer does better than they do. I worry that such writing may, in fact, encourage writers to indulge such feelings although the author does also present some excellent advice about avoiding the pitfall: "Just one thing saves me from envy: returning to my work. My desk is a quiet place. My hours there are like panes of clear glass."

My own experience of these problems is that it is all too easy to become focused on the injustices or the simple stupidities that surround the world of publishing, grants, literary prizes, and so on, but that when I do, I quickly lose my ability to write (and possibly even to think). Rejection letters, mistakes by agents, typos in published work, can all drive me crazy if I let them. But I know, too, that it is possible to turn away from the obsessions invited by such events (and by the myths that tell me I should obsess about them). I know it is possible to be pleased at the success of other writers, including those who are my friends, and I think too much is made of the pangs of envy that sometimes arrive along with the news of someone else's grant or someone else's big advance. Wouldn't you rather be someone who celebrates your friends' successes than someone who goes into a decline over them? By rejecting the myth and your own tendencies toward envy, you can empower yourself to stay conscious, get on with your work, and be a better friend as well.

Rejection letters are the subject of endless stories. Personally, I like the tales that make fun of the editors—editors who write ridiculous comments or explain pompously what you did wrong, or who are illiterate or unbearably rude. But I don't like the ones that make fun of the writer—usually playing up her extreme fragility, her neurotic self-doubt, or her major nervous breakdown, all of which can supposedly be triggered by a simple printed slip that says "No thank you."

Many writers have given good advice about submitting

work, usually suggesting that you cultivate a professional attitude that helps circumvent painful feelings of rejection. The way I do this, for work that is not handled by my agent, is to create a submission plan once I have a piece that's ready to go out. The plan includes five or six magazines or other suitable publication possibilities, and assumes that when the piece is rejected by the first, I will immediately send it on to the next. That way, resubmitting becomes simply a task, not a major crisis.

Of course the myths contain grains of truth: writers *do* feel hurt by rejection; writers *do* seek to cushion our sensibilities with drugs, cigarettes, alcohol, family melodramas, barrel loads of M&M's, television, bad relationships, or whatever we happen to have a penchant for. We live, after all, in a world that offers more and more opportunities for escapism of the deadening variety, and writing memoirs can lead to painful places—places we don't want to stay in too long. We want to go there, but we don't want it to hurt too much. That's why the romantic myths get to us, whispering that the bottle or the candy bars will make it all much easier.

What we really need, of course, are new images of what it means to be a writer: images that include healthy food, exercise, a sane attitude, and a tranquil soul—all of which are surely more compatible with great writing than is being a physical and mental wreck. We need to encourage one another in these directions and reject the old stereotypes; we must remind one another that fighting with our families or suffering through a love affair that denigrates us are not essential pastimes for a writer. After all, writing itself is hard enough without adding alcoholism, drug addiction and angst to the qualifications. There is no evidence that good writing requires any of them. What writing does require is that we nurture the stamina it takes to work hard and that we stay fully conscious—and alive.

❶ Write no more than four pages that describe your own encounters with the myths that surround writers and writing, or with people who embodied those myths (family members, teachers, friends, writers at their readings, writers you've read about, etc.).

❷ Outline an ideal working day in the life of a writer, free of the old stereotypes and using new and healthier visions of what it means to be a writer. Use first person or create an imaginary character.

❸ Invent a conversation in which you and another writer (real or imaginary) discuss how you deal with publication, rejection, competition, and other related issues. It's fine to disagree, argue, change your mind, or change the other person's mind!

12

*Getting
Feedback
on Your
Work*

A rtists have always tended to hang out together. Groups of writers met at certain cafés; artists of all kinds gathered at famous "salons." The Paris expatriates, the Bloomsbury group, the Black Mountain poets, and the members of numerous other literary circles offered one another company, support, argument, and sometimes serious, helpful criticism. Most of these "schools" had a large number of the privileged in their ranks. There were few women and even fewer people of color (with the exception of the Harlem Renaissance writers, among whom were few women), primarily because the lifestyle favored those who had independent incomes and who, if they had children, had either a wife or a paid caretaker to take care of them.

Today, writing programs, workshops, and informal writing groups offer some of the same benefits but to a much wider range of participants. Although workshops still overwhelmingly attract white, middle-class students, a few are making more than token efforts at outreach. By virtue of being free of charge, however, local peer writing groups offer the greatest opportunity for most writers, including the experienced and published, the inexperienced, those with few resources, and those who are outside the mainstream and lack the confidence to apply to a workshop.

Writing groups also have the advantage that they can be any size (from two to about twelve) and that anyone can start one. If you don't hear about a group and if you have no writer friends, put up a notice in a place where you think writers might hang out, or make a flyer you can hand out at a local reading. Soon you will find like-minded people. If you live in a rural area where there are no other writers, investigate the Internet or try to connect by mail with at least one other writer. Sometimes it is worth traveling to the nearest college to take a creative writing class, just to find a few people with whom you can continue to meet or correspond after the class is over.

Getting feedback on your drafts is an invaluable part of the process. Memoir, in particular, can be difficult for you to read dispassionately. Since you are writing from experience, you may find it hard to know if what you have put on the page makes sense to the reader. You may think things are clear when they are not, because of all the background information you alone have. The tone, too, may be hard for you to judge. Sometimes your emotional investment in the story is such that old feelings rise up to color the voice and tone; you may not realize when you have temporarily lost the consistency of your narrative voice. As in other kinds of creative writing, the structure and the language of your memoir can always benefit from the good editorial eye of an outside reader.

Another pitfall particular to the memoir is the temptation to drop your standards, both as writer and critiquer, when the story involves surviving great hardship, as if the difficulty of the life itself somehow makes up for a lack of literary merit. As Nancy Mairs has pointed out, "It is not enough, from a literary point of view, to have had A Very Bad Experience (or, for that matter, A Very Good Experience) and lived to tell the tale. Illness, disability and death can, and must, provide no proof against rigorous aesthetic judgment." Or as V.S. Pritchett said, "It's all in the art. You get no credit for living."

Writing groups can encounter problems when the group does not have a preagreed structure and a reliable way to keep to that structure. Discussions can get way off the point, meetings can become social rather than work oriented, and group members can get to know each other so well that they lose their ability to look at the writing as writing, seeing instead another aspect of the person they have come to know. Although the members of a group may initially like the informality of a loose structure—it may seem less intimidating than a serious critique group—ultimately they become frustrated with how little it is helping their work. I have seen numerous groups meet for a few months and then break up in dissatisfaction because they were unwilling to adopt a format that helped them focus on the task at hand.

For many years, I have directed the Flight of the Mind annual summer workshops for women writers, at which participants are encouraged to form peer critique groups in addition to the classes led by established writers. Over the years, I have developed a set of guidelines to help such groups stay on track. With input from several other writers who have taught at the workshops, especially Valerie Miner, these guidelines now serve a large number of critique groups around the country. You will find them at the end of this chapter.

If you become part of a writing group that uses these guidelines, or even if you decide, as I did while writing this book, simply to meet regularly with one writer friend and swap drafts—you will go home from meetings with lots of notes on your manuscript. If there are many suggestions for improvement, you should feel encouraged, even elated: if you do not, either your writing group is not functioning as it should, or you are not being receptive to the support it offers in its criticism.

Soon after the meeting, you should sit down with all the

various comments and go through the piece. I find it useful to "try out" all except the comments I feel certain are way off the mark (and even those are worth revisiting later, so I don't throw them away). Even if I am doubtful, it doesn't hurt to make a change on the computer, or by hand in a notebook, and see how I like it. Often I will go back to my original version. Sometimes the suggestion will not be to my liking but will lead me on to a further change I might not have thought of. Many comments, however, do lead to immediate changes: inconsistencies that one reader may have caught, for instance, such as a character in your story wearing brown suede shoes on one page and wellington boots on the next; or spelling and grammar corrections.

Learning to make use of good critique is one of the most important skills a writer can develop. When you come to work with editors, it will greatly improve the quality of your published work if you are receptive to their suggestions, rather than protective of your work to the point of obstinacy when good help is available. A good working relationship with an editor can be an exciting and informative experience and a great gift.

Neither editors nor peer groups, however, are guaranteed to provide only good critique: some members of your group may be inexperienced or unable to see the writing for the content. What is not useful, you can let go. There is no need, in a group at least, to argue for your work: it is always and forever *yours*. No matter what anyone says, the decisions are *yours*. You should not take up group time explaining why you don't agree, and you don't have to explain or justify your final decisions, no matter how hard your group may have pushed you to make changes.

Being good at receiving feedback is a skill that can sometimes take your work to a level you might not have reached alone. But trusting your own judgment is, in the long run, even more important. This is *your* story. Only *you* can write it.

Read these aloud slowly, point by point, and discuss them at your first meeting. Agree to follow them, or amend them in a way that suits your group, and then stick to them.

Decide if you are going to send your work to all the group members ahead of time, which allows more work to be discussed at the meeting or if you prefer to read the work silently or aloud at the meeting—a practice that works better for poetry and other short pieces than for longer fiction or nonfiction pieces.

All members of a writing group should be actively writing. Although members can go through "dry" periods, a group should not have members who only critique and never bring their own work.

Good critique cannot happen without *both* parties (those giving critique and those whose work is under discussion) playing their part successfully. It is as important to be good at receiving a critique of your work as it is to be able to give it.

The process will not happen spontaneously; it has to be learned. Our instincts may be, variously, to say what's wrong, to praise to the hilt, to remain silent, to argue every point, or simply to try and say what each person wants to hear. We may be instinctively a great critic but a terrible subject or vice versa. We all, undoubtedly, have strong points and weak ones in the critique process. Instincts should be tempered with caution and a willingness to learn new responses.

➤When Your Work Is on the Table

DO NOT:

• Say how bad, unfinished, trivial, or unworthy it is.

• Explain your intention in writing it (if it works your intention will be apparent).

• Tell us exactly where and how you wrote it ("on the bus going to work I saw this woman...").

• Respond *at all* until everyone has commented. This means you remain silent throughout the critique.

BUT DO:

• Ask for the specific feedback you would like.

• Make notes on your copy as people talk—even if you don't immediately agree with what they say.

➤When Someone Else's Work Is on the Table

DO NOT:

• Criticize in a way that will make the writer feel stupid or insulted (be respectful).

• Make sweeping judgments ("this is good"; "this is bad") but give personal specific responses using "I" ("I was moved by the last section; "I was confused at the top of page 3").

• Tell stories from your own experience that the work in question reminds you of (this is not about you).

• Assume that an "I" character is the writer. Even if the writing is memoir, refer to the "I" character as "the speaker" or "the narrator," rather than as "you". (See "The Narrator," page 25).

Be sure the facilitator reminds people of this rule if they start using "you."

• Try to make major changes, reword in your own words, or impose your own view. Your job is to help the writer convey his or her own view powerfully.

• Expound on a point that has already been clearly made. You can say you agree or simply pass.

BUT DO:

• Try to believe in the possibilities of each piece. (You might want to read "The Doubting Game and the Believing Game" in Peter Elbow's *Writing Without Teachers* for more about this.)

• Articulate your response as clearly as you can—it is not enough simply to feel something. Good critique depends on your making conscious and articulating your responses.

• Tell them what you liked, what moved you, what you can still see or feel. (These positive responses should come first.)

• Tell the writer what you remember most clearly.

• Tell them where you lost attention or were confused.

• Write notes on your copy of their work if you like and give it to the writer (this is often useful later and saves time in the critique group). This is particularly suitable for grammar, punctuation, spelling correction, etc.

▶Suggested Process

Each group meeting should have one person who facilitates, keeps time, and draws attention if things go off track. This job should be rotated: it should not be the same person for more than one meeting. If your meetings also rotate their location, you may simply have the person whose house it is at be the facilitator. At any rate, decide on the next facilitator at the end of each meeting before the group evaluation. The facilitator should read through these guidelines (or the amended ones agreed on by the group) before the meeting. He or she should not hesitate to point out if the group is getting off track.

At the beginning of the meeting, divide up the time realistically. If there is more work to be critiqued than can possibly fit, make a commitment to some of it for the next meeting. Allocate equal time to each piece of work and stick to the time limit. If you run out of time before everyone has had a chance to speak, have the remaining members write down any comments that haven't already been covered and give them to the writer. Do not allow extra time. It may seem necessary, but almost always it is not.

Read the piece of work, if you have not already done so ahead of time.

Go around the circle with each person speaking in turn. This is the best way to ensure equal participation in a new group. You may be able to move on to random turns later, but if this allows people to ramble or to repeat one another, or if some people speak all the time, go back to taking turns. Do not repeat what has been said before, but be content to simply state your agreement and pass.

Do not jump into a discussion when it is not your turn, but wait for each writer to speak. If discussion on a particular point seems desirable, it should happen *after* everyone has spoken.

The writer should not respond but listen. This is very important. In order to help this happen, do not address direct questions to the writer. He or she will learn more from listening to the rest of you discuss something you are not clear about, than from clarifying it for you. You may invite him or her to respond briefly after everyone has finished the critique.

Allow five minutes, or whatever is necessary, at the end to evaluate the session. Again, each person should speak in turn. Decide on the facilitator for the next meeting before doing the evaluation, so that person can take notes about what worked well and what needs to be improved.

APPENDIX
Your Memoir and the Law

Many writers engaged in writing memoir worry about being sued. For most, this is a way of focusing their fear of telling the truth. It is a legitimate legal concern for only a very few.

The chances of your being sued are extremely small—it practically never happens. Aside from the question of whether there are legal grounds for a lawsuit, there are two very good reasons why you are unlikely to face a legal challenge. First of all, it is very expensive to bring a lawsuit—so expensive, in fact, that it is beyond the means of most people (though hiring a lawyer to threaten a lawsuit is within the means of more). Even when a lawyer is paid not on an hourly basis but with a percentage of the amount won in the suit, the person suing will have to pay a lot of expenses such as filing fees, expert witness fees, depositions, and so on. Secondly, most people who may dislike your version of events or your portrayal of them do not want to bring even more attention to what you have said, although the lawsuit gives them the opportunity to refute it.

I strongly encourage you not to worry about your legal situation while you are writing your memoir. The time to consider it is when you are ready to publish. In fact, finding a publisher will help you get a realistic sense of whether or not there is anything to worry about because your publisher will be concerned about any possible legal action. Most publishing contracts require you to indemnify your publisher against any claims of defamation or invasion of privacy, which means that if they are sued, you will have to pay. However, no publisher wants to rely on collecting from an author in such a situation; they will consult their own legal counsel to make sure there are no potential problems. It's certainly a good idea, once a manuscript has been accepted for publication, to talk over with your editor any concerns you have and, if there are any real problems, work out solutions together.

It's also a good idea to have some understanding of the relevant laws. I give below some selected and simplified facts about the laws that might apply to your memoir. There are, of course, many subtleties in addition to what is outlined here. If you want to explore it further, go to your local library and find a book that relates to the legal aspects of publishing.

Mostly the law reinforces what you already know as a responsible writer: you need to stick to the truth, and you need to be meticulous about your facts when someone else's reputation could be harmed. (Under defamation laws, for instance, a statement that is true is not defamatory, no matter how damaging it might be to someone's reputation.) You need to use facts fairly and not manipulate them. (Invasion of privacy laws protect people from being portrayed in a false light.)

❧ ❧ ❧

There are two general areas of the law that apply to your writing: **defamation** and **invasion of privacy**.

Defamation laws, which include libel (written defamation) and slander (spoken defamation), are concerned with the publication of false information about a person that causes damage to his or her reputation and/or ability to succeed in a business. Classic examples include statements regarding criminal conduct, gross immorality, bankruptcy or insolvency, Ku Klux Klan membership, etc.

Invasion of Privacy/Protection of Personality Rights are concerned mainly with the publication of offensive, embarrassing, or misleading facts about a person, and with the unfair exploitation, for profit, of someone's image or name.

These are civil laws—not criminal laws—under which the person claiming to be harmed by your writing must bring a civil lawsuit against you. This means that the person who feels harmed will have to hire a lawyer rather than use the free services of a district attorney. Since these are not criminal laws, there are no criminal penalties. The lawsuit will be about compensation or stopping the dissemination of your memoir, or both.

These are the main things you need to know about each area:

DEFAMATION

To be legally ruled defamatory, a statement in your memoir must be:

• **False**. A statement that can be proved true is not defamatory.

• **Published**. The statement must be communicated publicly.

• **Stated as fact**. Statements that clearly represent an opinion rather than a fact are relatively safe from defamation suits.

• **About a named or identifiable person**. Your statement is considered defamatory only when the person is named or recognizable because of his or her personality, physical description, or other identifying characteristics. Defamation can also be claimed by groups when your statement can be shown to injure a whole group or one of its members.

•**About a living person**. Generally speaking, no one can sue you on behalf of a dead person.

•**Damaging or injurious to the person concerned**. For it to be defamatory, your statement must cause the person to be held in public contempt or hatred, or must interfere with her or his ability to succeed financially or professionally, or must cause her or him to lose a spouse. These injuries are often presumed without the person concerned having to prove them.

You should also bear in mind that legally different standards are set for how *public* and *private* people are written about. As an author, you have more freedom to comment on the lives of public officials or public figures such as entertainers, activists, corporate officers, political candidates, and others who "thrust themselves or their ideas into the public eye."

A public person bringing a lawsuit against you would have to prove that you made defamatory statements with what is called "actual malice." An example of actual malice is that you knew your statement to be untrue or you didn't care whether it was true or not. Private people, however, do not have to prove such malice; they can win their case simply by proving you were careless or inattentive in researching or verifying your statements about them.

INVASION OF PRIVACY/PROTECTION OF PERSONALITY RIGHTS

"Invasion of privacy" is an umbrella concept that can encompass several quite different situations that would apply to a memoirist:

•**The publication of offensive or embarrassing private facts about an identifiable person**—facts that are not already a matter of public record. The definition of what is offensive or embarrassing is based on the "community standards" of your locale.

•**Using facts in a way that conveys a person in a false light.** This is different from defamation in that here the facts are used to mislead, though the facts may be true.

•**Using someone's name or picture for commercial gain without consent.** For example, if someone about whom you write in your memoir is famous or has a proprietary, money-making interest in her or his name, image, photographic likeness, etc., you should be cautious about using any of those in your memoir if you plan to publish it for profit. In such cases, it's a good idea to get written permission.

A key element of privacy laws is the "newsworthy" standard, which allows you to publish facts about someone that are deemed of legitimate public interest.

Under these laws, public officials and public figures do not have a right to privacy except in areas that have no connection to their public role. You cannot, however, use their name or picture for commercial gain without their permission, nor can you employ invasive fact-gathering with such people.

Again, bearing in mind that the likelihood of anyone suing is extremely low, there are nevertheless precautions you can take:

•**Tell the truth.** Since it may be difficult to prove in some instances, wherever possible research your facts and keep accurate records of your research. Especially when making accusations against people, make sure you have hard evidence to back your claims.

•**Express your opinions as opinions.** Be careful not to state opinions as facts.

•**Attribute controversial statements to others**. If sources other than you can verify your version of a story that might provoke someone, it is good to quote such sources, particularly if they are known to be reliable. However, you are still ultimately responsible for what you say and phrases such as "it is alleged" are unlikely to protect you if you make questionable statements.

- **Get consent from those you write about**. Getting a release (written permission) if you can is a very good idea. Consult a good writer's legal resource for examples. I recommend a book by Brad Bunnin and Peter Beren, *The Writer's Legal Companion.*

- **Change names and disguise people**. If you are worried about the consequences, legal or otherwise, of publishing a story that might upset someone, making them unrecognizable is a good way to go.

- **Don't worry forever**. There is a statute of limitations that varies from state to state—generally one or two years from the date of publication, after which you cannot be sued.

Now that you have read this, go ahead and forget about it until your memoir is written and ready to be published. Do not allow yourself to refer to it while you are writing, and do not confuse your nervousness about telling your story with the unlikely possibility of legal consequences. Writing and publishing are two separate stages of a writer's work. Deal with them one at a time.

Permissions Acknowledgments

Index to Authors and Titles

About the Author

JUDITH BARRINGTON is the author of a full-length memoir, *Lifesaving*, and many shorter memoirs that have been published in literary magazines including *Sonora Review* (Annual Nonfiction Award, 1993), *The American Voice*, and *Left Bank*, and anthologies including *The Stories That Shape Us: Contemporary Women Write About the West*, edited by Teresa Jordan and James Hepworth; *The House on Via Gombito: Writing by North American Women Abroad*, edited by Madelon Sprengnether and C.W. Truesdale; *Uncommon Waters: Women Write About Fishing*, edited by Holly Morris; and *Loss of the Ground Note: Women Writing About the Loss of Their Mothers*, edited by Helen Vozenilek. Her memoir, "Poetry and Prejudice" won the 1995 Andres Berger Award for Creative Nonfiction. She is the author of two volumes of poetry, each of which contains a memoir: *Trying to Be an Honest Woman* and *History and Geography* .

She has taught creative writing for the past fifteen years at many colleges and universities, including Portland State University, Lewis & Clark College, and Washington State University, and at the summer writing workshops Haystack and Fishtrap. She taught for twelve years in the Arts in Education programs of Oregon and Washington. She is director and faculty member of the Flight of the Mind Summer Writing Workshops for Women and Flight of the Mind, Mexico.

ORDERING INFORMATION

Eighth Mountain books can be found in independent and chain bookstores across the U.S., Canada, Great Britain, and Australia. If your favorite bookstore is out of the title you want, ask them to order it for you. You can also order books directly from Eighth Mountain for destinations in the U.S. or Canada. Please add $2.50 for the first book ($3.50 in Canada) and 50¢ each additional book for postage and handling. Send a check payable in U.S. dollars to the Eighth Mountain Press. Books will be mailed book rate. If you need speedier delivery, call us to discuss other options.

Eighth Mountain titles are distributed to the trade by Consortium Book Sales and Distribution, 1045 Westgate Drive, Saint Paul, MN 55114-1065 (800/283-3572 or 612/221-9035) and are carried by all major book wholesalers and library jobbers.

For specialty, bulk, and catalog sales contact the Eighth Mountain Press directly.

The Eighth Mountain Press
624 SE 29th Avenue
Portland, OR 97214
phone: 503/233-3936
fax: 503/233-0774